VGM Opportunities Series

OPPORTUNITIES IN DENTAL CARE CAREERS

Bonnie L. Kendall

Revised by
Blythe Camenson

Foreword by
Elizabeth C. Sidney
Editor
American Dental Assistants Association

VGM Career Books
NTC/Contemporary Publishing Group

Library of Congress Cataloging-in-Publication Data

Kendall, Bonnie L.
  Opportunities in dental care careers / Bonnie L. Kendall ; foreword by Elizabeth C. Sidney.—
Rev. ed. / by Blythe Camenson
    p.   cm. — (VGM opportunities series)
  Includes bibliographical references.
  ISBN 0-658-00477-8 (cloth) — ISBN 0-658-00478-6 (pbk.)
  1. Dentistry—Vocational guidance. I. Title. II. Series

RK60 .K44   2000
617.6'023—dc21
                                                                    00-39273

Published by VGM Career Books
A division of NTC/Contemporary Publishing Group, Inc.
4255 West Touhy Avenue, Lincolnwood (Chicago), Illinois 60712-1975 U.S.A.
Copyright © 2001 by NTC/Contemporary Publishing Group
International Standard Book Number: 0-658-00477-8 (cloth)
                                    0-658-00478-6 (paper)

01   02   03   04   05   06   LB   15   14   13   12   11   10   9   8   7   6   5   4   3   2

CONTENTS

Ancient dental practices. Dentistry in the Middle Ages. Founder of modern dentistry. Dentistry in the United States. History of dental hygiene. History of dental assisting. History of dental laboratory technology. Dental associations.

General practice office. Dental hygienist. Dental assistant. Dental laboratory technician. Receptionist. Daily routine. The dental office. Choosing employees. Communicating with patients. Recordkeeping. Professional advisors. Quality of care.

Dental public health. Endodontics. Oral pathology. Oral and maxillofacial surgery. Orthodontics. Pediatric dentistry. Periodontics. Prosthodontics. General practitioner. Federal dental services. Public service careers. The role of dental research. Salaries for dentists.

ABOUT THE AUTHOR

Bonnie L. Kendall is an editor and writer who has concentrated on both dental and medical subjects. She was the editorial director for *The Journal of the American Dental Association.*

A native of Cambridge, Ohio, Mrs. Kendall received her degree in journalism from Ohio State University and did graduate work at Ohio University, Athens, Ohio. She has been a freelance editor for several medical publications in the Chicago area. She has written several articles related to dentistry: "Consumer Education in Dental Health," "New Technology for Dental Care," and "Editing for the Dental Profession." She has also presented workshops at the American Medical Writers Association meetings and at the American Dental Association annual session in Washington, DC.

Mrs. Kendall lives in Downers Grove, Illinois, with her husband, David, a freelance photographer. They have been active in many civic organizations, including Boy Scouts, public school committees, and a school for handicapped children and adults. Traveling to Great Britain is their favorite hobby.

This edition has been thoroughly revised by Blythe Camenson, a full-time writer of career books. Camenson's main concern is helping job seekers make educated choices. She firmly believes that with enough information, readers can find long-term, satisfying careers.

Camenson's interests range from history and photography to writing novels. She is also director of Fiction Writer's Connection, a membership organization whose function is to help new writers improve their craft and learn the ropes to getting published. Her website can be found at www.fictionwriters.com.

Camenson has more than three dozen books in print, most of which have been published by VGM Career Books. She is also the co-author of *Your Novel Proposal: From Creation to Contract* (Writer's Digest Books, 1999).

She was educated in Boston, earning her B.A. in English and psychology from the University of Massachusetts and her M.Ed. in counseling from Northeastern University.

FOREWORD

When you choose to enter the dental care field, you will need many skills. Academic ability and a willingness to work hard are only the beginning. Because dental professionals work with people of all backgrounds and ages, they must also be able to communicate with and show concern for all their patients. They need knowledge, skill, patience, and commitment to their careers.

As you investigate careers in dental care, the number of possibilities may surprise you. Jobs and specialties are numerous. Modern dental care requires the combined efforts of dental assistants, dental hygienists, dentists, dental laboratory technicians, and dental researchers. These professionals specialize in everything from pediatric dentistry to oral pathology.

Dental care is a growing field. Today, people are more aware than ever before of the need for preventative dentistry. Elementary schools educate children about the importance of dental care. Magazine and newspaper articles remind readers of the need for regular dental visits. Also, many more people have dental insurance than in the past, thus ensuring that dentists will have more patients. As the population ages, the demand for geriatric dentistry will rise too. Cosmetic dentistry is another rapidly growing and expanding area.

If you pursue a career in dental care, you will become a valued resource in your community. You will be joining the ranks of respected professionals whose work allows others to enjoy good health.

Elizabeth C. Sidney
Editor
American Dental Assistants Association

PREFACE

"Brush your teeth or they'll rot and fall out of your head!"

How many times have we heard that, both on the receiving end as children and on the giving end as adults? Well, today it's unlikely that *all* your teeth would fall out without regular dental care, but with proper oral hygiene and faithful visits to a competent dentist, many children are unlikely to get cavities, and most adults are unlikely to end up with dentures.

There are several reasons for the improved state of dental health. For one, the science of dentistry over recent decades has made enormous changes in delivery and types of treatment. Years past, a dentist worked alone. But today the dental office is staffed with a team of dental professionals that generally includes, in addition to the dentist, a dental hygienist, dental assistant, sometimes a laboratory assistant, and a receptionist. Also, new specialties have emerged, and established specialties continue to grow, which add to the services this field has to offer.

Concurrent with this change in dental office makeup is the fact that today people care more about their teeth than ever before. Over the years, the emphasis in dentistry has become one of prevention. As we take better care of our teeth, under the guidance of the dentist and his or her dental team, a visit to the dentist's office—though not necessarily a pleasant experience—need not be a torturous ordeal.

Modern techniques and materials at the dentist's disposal help make teeth stronger, more attractive, and apt to last a lifetime. Dentistry today is not just a matter of "pulling teeth." It involves diagnosing, treating, and preventing diseases of the teeth, gums, and jaws; cleaning teeth; and teaching patients about proper oral hygiene as well as helping them establish good nutritional eating habits to help keep teeth and gums strong. It's easy to see why a career in this field can offer so many interesting options to those attracted to it.

If you decide to enter the field of dental care, you will join a prestigious group of more than four million people in health careers. You will be concerned with much more than the state of the patient's mouth. You will be actively involved with the health care of your patients.

You will be concerned with the education of patients in preventive dentistry. You will be involved with children, adults, elderly patients, and patients with special needs. You will work long hours in training and on the job, but you will have the security in your profession and pride in your accomplishments.

If you're interested in any of the various jobs the field of dentistry has to offer, *Opportunities in Dental Care Careers* will give you a clear picture of what to expect as you pursue a career as a dentist, dental hygienist, laboratory technician, endodontist, orthodontist, pediatric dentist, or any of the many other areas there are to choose from. You'll also learn what it's like to deal with different patient populations, how much money you can expect to make over your years of practice, the educational requirements of your area of interest, and the associations and other professional organizations that are there to support you. Good luck as you find your place in this exciting and rewarding profession.

ACKNOWLEDGMENTS

This book about the people who practice dentistry could not have been written without the help of my friends and colleagues at the American Dental Association who supplied me with facts, figures, and feelings about the profession of dentistry.

I have learned much as I have written this book, especially from those contributors to *The Journal of the American Dental Association* who have shared their pride and their knowledge about their profession.

CHAPTER 1

HISTORY OF DENTISTRY

The profession of dentistry with its allied careers is concerned with a specialized area within the healing arts: maintaining the health of the teeth and gums and other tissues in the mouth. Dentistry offers a variety of career opportunities within this health care field.

Opportunities include the careers of dental assistants, dental hygienists, dental laboratory technicians, general practitioners, and specialists such as orthodontists, oral surgeons, pediatric dentists, and others. Each career requires a different specialization or level of training and education, but all require skill, precision, and concern for the patients who need dental care.

ANCIENT DENTAL PRACTICES

Dentistry was not recognized as a separate and distinct profession until the eighteenth century, but many dental procedures have existed for four to five thousand years. Some practices go back to the Egyptian empire of 2000 B.C., where medicine was a profession in which a physician's work was limited to one area of the body. Some of these physicians dealt with the teeth and mouth.

Ancient papyrus records show that Egyptians had remedies for toothaches, such as stone powder, ocher (iron ore), and honey. A tooth powder for "strengthening" teeth was described as resin, ocher, and malachite (a copper mixture).

Egyptian physicians practiced little restorative dentistry except to use wires to secure loosened teeth. They also extracted teeth. Oral hygiene was a common practice, as a sign, or hieroglyph, for "washing the mouth" was often found on papyrus records.

In ancient India and China, groups of physicians made up a professional class and training was provided for students. Use of a toothbrush was recommended in medical writings; the toothbrush was a twig with its end frayed to provide bristles. The tongue was scraped with a metal scraper, and toothpicks were used.

Chinese physicians used acupuncture (use of needles to relieve pain) in treating nearly every disease, including diseases of the mouth. In the Chinese civilization and others, a tooth worm was thought to be responsible for decay—a superstition that persisted through the Middle Ages in Europe.

Both in China and in Central and South America, decorating teeth was a common practice. The Chinese used gold to make covers for their teeth. The Aztec and Mayan Indians inserted semiprecious stones such as turquoise and jade into their teeth.

Many remedies for toothache consisted of medicines made from plants: cloves, pepper, cinnamon, poppy seeds, ginger, copal (resin from trees), mint, and tobacco. Many of these treatments were combined with special incantations, or poems, to make the remedy more effective.

Greek-Roman Dentistry

The Greek physician Hippocrates, who lived about the fifth century B.C., raised the art of medicine to a higher level. A school based on his writings and teachings was established. Thirty-two paragraphs in Hippocrates' books were devoted to dental treatment; a numbering system for teeth was devised.

Hippocrates advised extraction of teeth only if they were both decayed and weak. For decayed teeth, it was recommended that a red-hot wire be inserted into the tooth to cauterize the decay. Fractures or breaks in the jaw were treated by repositioning the bone and holding it in place with wire until healing occurred. To restore lost teeth, teeth were drilled and wires were passed through the holes and wound around the natural teeth.

Contact with Greek civilization helped carry dental knowledge into the Roman empire. Three groups of practitioners dealt with problems of teeth: the regular physician, the physician specializing in dentistry, and the technician. Teeth were extracted with forceps made of iron, which resembled today's pliers. Small drills were used to relieve pressure inside a tooth. Small sticks of mastic wood (from an evergreen tree) were used to clean teeth. Tooth powders were made of fine pumice, eggshell, and animal horn.

Restorative dentistry was largely learned from the work of the Etruscans. These people lived in central Italy and made numerous crowns and bridges for teeth that can be seen today in Italian museums. Gold bands were used to hold in place artificial teeth that had been removed from other humans or calves. In the prosperous days of the Roman empire, artificial teeth became important for appearance, and many restorative procedures were developed. Like many Greek and Roman discoveries, this important knowledge was lost as the Roman Empire disappeared.

DENTISTRY IN THE MIDDLE AGES

Many of the tools and techniques that were developed in early civilizations improved little during the Middle Ages. Dentistry and medicine made few advances. Doctors and surgeons were not skilled in treating dental diseases, and barber-surgeons were permitted to extract teeth. Knowledge was preserved mainly in monasteries, and monks became medical practitioners.

The chief dental remedy was removal of teeth. This was usually done by "tooth drawers," who came into medieval towns on market days and set up shop. They often wore a necklace of teeth to proclaim their trade, and they bragged about the painlessness of their methods.

Revival of Scientific Thought

In the early sixteenth century, interest was rekindled in scientific thought and methods. The study of the anatomy of the human body led to new discoveries about the mouth and teeth. Vesalius, a Flemish anatomist, described with some accuracy the parts of the teeth. An Italian anatomist, Eustachius, illustrated the development of teeth in all phases. He wrote one of the first books entirely devoted to dentistry.

A French dental pioneer, Paré, described methods for transplanting teeth, repairing fractures, and removing teeth. He recommended dental substitutes of bone held in place with wire. The Dutch inventor of the microscope, Leeuwenhoek, was the first to see the organisms that are found in the mouth. The work of all these scientists became known and could be shared with others because of the invention of printing and easy accessibility to their books.

FOUNDER OF MODERN DENTISTRY

This increasing knowledge about dentistry culminated in the work of a Frenchman, Pierre Fauchard, called the founder of modern dentistry. Fauchard practiced in Paris and began his training with a surgeon in the royal navy. His outstanding contribution to dentistry was his two-volume, 848-page book published in 1728. This book on dental information, *Le Chirurgien Dentiste, ou traité des dentes,* proved to be an authoritative guide for more than a hundred years.

In preparing his book, Fauchard summarized all the then available knowledge about dental anatomy, treatment of diseases, extraction and replacement of teeth, construction of dentures, and irregularities of teeth.

Fauchard shared his knowledge and research with colleagues. This concept of sharing information helped to transform the dentist from a skilled artisan to a practitioner of the healing arts.

The work of Fauchard led many others in England and western Europe to publish their studies on such topics as care of teeth, their structures, and diseases. With this new interest in the practice of dentistry as a separate profession, distinct from the medical profession, the foundation was laid for the practice of preventive and restorative dentistry as it is known today.

DENTISTRY IN THE UNITED STATES

The emphasis on restorative dentistry found its way to the American colonies. In America, early advertisements by surgeon-dentists (as they were then called) offered transplants of teeth, artificial teeth, and dentifrice (liquid, paste, or powder for cleaning teeth and gums). Many of these practitioners traveled a regular circuit from town to town, announcing their arrival in local newspapers.

As the population increased and larger towns and cities were established, dentists began to practice in one location. Sometimes other occupations were combined with dental practice. A famous Revolutionary hero and silversmith, Paul Revere, also made artificial teeth and inserted them. Other practitioners began to specialize and to make improvements in existing techniques and tools.

Two discoveries contributed a great deal to the progress of dentistry: anesthesia and radiography. Anesthesia was first used by Dr. Horace Wells of Connecticut in 1844 when he instructed a patient to inhale nitrous oxide before a tooth was extracted. In 1895, in Germany, William Roentgen made the discovery of the X-ray.

Dr. C. Edmund Kells, New Orleans, is credited as the first dentist in the United States to use an X-ray machine in making radiographs of teeth. With radiographs, dentists could detect which teeth should be removed and which could be left safely in the mouth. Both discoveries eliminated a great deal of pain previously associated with dentistry.

First United States Dental School

The first independent dental school in the United States—the Baltimore College of Dental Surgery—opened in 1840. Before that time, the apprenticeship system for education of dentists was used. It was customary for anyone, with or without formal education, to become a dentist by serving five years of apprenticeship. After those five years, the individual could practice as a qualified dentist. However, the kind of training that was received depended entirely on the knowledge and skill of the dentist with whom the individual was associated. In some instances, training was of acceptable quality; in others, it was not.

Formal training at the Baltimore College of Dental Surgery consisted of two full courses of lectures for four months, in addition to performing certain dental operations and preparing and setting artificial teeth. A thesis on some aspect of dentistry was also required. If the candidates were found competent after examination by the faculty members (four teachers), they were then awarded the degree of Doctor of Dental Surgery, the first use of the now-familiar D.D.S.

From this first dental school, a system of accredited dental schools, each associated with a college or university, has evolved. There are currently approximately fifty-five such programs that offer modern dental health education for dentists, some of which offer the Doctor of Medical Dentistry (D.M.D.) degree.

Today's health-care offices include not only the services of the dentist but also those of the dental hygienist, dental assistant, and laboratory technician. For many years, dentists worked alone, performing nearly all of the functions needed in the office; gradually the concept of an organized dental team developed.

HISTORY OF DENTAL HYGIENE

Dental hygiene, as a separate function, is more than seventy-five years old; however, the concept is older. It could be said that the concept of oral care began when oral hygiene was practiced by ancient Egyptians.

Many dentists in the late 1800s and early 1900s practiced preventive dentistry by performing thorough cleaning in the dental office. This proved beneficial to patients but time-consuming to dentists.

One of the first dentists to employ a hygienist in a dental office was Dr. Alfred Fones of Bridgeport, Connecticut. In 1906, he trained his office assistant, Mrs. Irene Newman, in both oral cleaning and dental health education. In 1913, through his efforts, the city of Bridgeport appropriated five thousand dollars to start an educational program, developed by Dr. Fones, in the city schools.

The school was located next to Dr. Fones's office; thirty-three young women entered the program. The faculty members were dentists from the area and instructors for dental and medical schools.

From this first class (which included schoolteachers, nurses, and dental assistants), ten hygienists were employed by the city of Bridgeport. A health-education program was started in which the new dental hygienists presented classroom talks and training. Programs for parents were sponsored. The hygienists performed cleaning functions for the schoolchildren and kept dental records for them. In collecting the data, these hygienists developed the first dental public health program.

The first courses at the Fones school were so successful that three more schools were started, two in New York and one in Massachusetts. The second school was started in 1916 by Dr. Louise Ball, the New York School of Dental Hygiene, which is now a department of the College of Dental Surgery of Columbia University. Another school was started at the Eastman Dental Dispensary in Rochester, New York, and another at the Forsyth Dental Dispensary for Children in Boston, Massachusetts.

Only fourteen more schools were started between 1913 and 1946. But since 1946, the number has increased rapidly. Currently, there are approximately two hundred training programs to meet the demand for the services of dental hygienists.

A committee from the American Dental Association in 1946 set requirements for existing schools of dental hygiene so that each school could offer similar basic programs. After the required courses are offered, each school is able to vary its programs as needed.

By 1951, dental hygienists were licensed in all states. At first dental hygienists were almost exclusively women, but the first man was licensed in the late 1950s in Oregon.

As education and training have advanced, the duties of the hygienist have changed. In all states, the hygienist is licensed to perform functions related to cleaning and education, but, in some states, the hygienist can perform expanded functions related to placement of fillings and administration of anesthesia.

HISTORY OF DENTAL ASSISTING

The man who pioneered the use of dental X-rays, Dr. C. Edmund Kells, was the first to hire a woman as an assistant. Men had been working as assistants, often as apprentices, in 1885, but this was a daring change. At that time, a woman did not come alone to a dental office for treatment; she was accompanied by her husband or a companion.

After Dr. Kells's practice prospered, other dentists began to hire female assistants. The sign "Lady in Attendance" was placed in the windows of many dental offices, and women felt more comfortable entering these offices alone. Slowly, more and more women were hired.

While many assistants were trained on the job, gradually, formal training programs were established. In the 1940s, the Education Committee of the American Dental Assistants Association outlined the first basic course of study.

The plan provided for a 104-hour course of study on subjects pertaining to dental procedures. In 1954, the University of North Carolina Dental School began a special correspondence school for dental assistants. By that time, the demand for assistants exceeded the supply, and more trained assistants were needed.

As more and more assistants were employed, their responsibilities increased. Although their duties include office management and clerical work, today many assistants work at chairside directly with patients. The assistants participate in technical procedures that do not directly require the professional knowledge and judgment of the dentist and improve the dentist's productivity and ability to provide more efficient dental care.

HISTORY OF DENTAL LABORATORY TECHNOLOGY

Some of the people who could be called the earliest laboratory technicians were silversmiths and goldsmiths who formed artificial teeth as a sideline to their work of sculpture, jewelry-making, and other crafts. These people worked either independently for a client or with a dentist to help solve a client's problem with artificial teeth or dentures.

In America during the nineteenth century, most dentists made artificial teeth and dentures or employed assistants or apprentices who helped in this work. The exact date when independent laboratories were started is not known. However, by the beginning of the twentieth century, many were established: In 1920 there were nearly 2,000 laboratories in the United States. Today there are about 9,500 in operation.

As in dentistry, a pattern of educating technicians from apprenticeship through training programs was developed. There are now approximately fifty accredited training programs, most of which are two-year programs. Many technicians are trained in the commercial laboratories; most laboratories require three-year programs.

To continue education and to share in new techniques and materials, technicians formed study groups. One such group was the Guild of Dental Craftsmen in New York. In 1945, more than eight hundred technicians attended a guild meeting at which technicians offered demonstrations of dental technology.

Today, the dental laboratory technician receives more formal education in all pertinent subjects through precise and scientific training.

DENTAL ASSOCIATIONS

The people who work in the dental health care field have formed associations for the advancement of the profession.

American Dental Association

The American Dental Association was founded in 1859 by a small group of dentists meeting in Niagara Falls, New York. However, the group split as a result of the Civil War, when the Southern Dental Association was formed. In 1897, the two groups united to form the National Dental Association. In 1922, the association again assumed its original and current name, the American Dental Association.

The objectives of the association are to encourage the improvement of the health of the public, to promote the art and science of dentistry, and to represent the interests of the members of the dental profession and the public it serves. Its current membership includes some 150,000 dentists and students.

The American Dental Association headquarters is in Chicago and contains the administrative agencies, a dental library, and a two-floor laboratory complex. In addition, a number of national allied dental organizations are located in the building.

The association has an office in Washington, DC, that works closely with Congress and other governmental agencies in the Washington area. For example, the ADA cooperates with the National Institute of Dental Research, which is part of the National Institutes of Health. Association staff members also do research work at the National Bureau of Standards and the National Library of Medicine.

Benefits of membership in the American Dental Association include many scientific, professional, and consumer publications and insurance programs. Each year a comprehensive scientific session is held.

In addition, the councils and bureaus of the association provide these services to members and to the public: formulating requirements for accreditation of educational programs, providing community dental health programs, evaluating dental materials and products, advising on laws relating to dental health, supplying data and statistics about the dental profession, and performing research in such areas as biochemistry, pharmacology, biology, and dental materials.

American Dental Hygienists' Association

A group of about fifty hygienists organized the American Dental Hygienists' Association at a meeting in Cleveland, Ohio, in 1923. By 1927 the association had 467 members. Growth of the association was slow during the depression years, but in the 1940s two factors contributed to a faster pace: during World War II, the military forces began accelerated programs for training dental hygienists, and more training programs were set up in technical institutes.

By 1960, there were thirty-seven training programs; the primary setting was the community college. The association worked to maintain high levels of education. By the end of the 1960s, nearly eighteen thousand hygienists were employed.

A major achievement of the association is setting and maintaining educational standards. The association (with the American Dental Association) provides continuing education for the practicing dental hygienist.

The association helps the hygienist keep up to date through publications, scientific sessions, workshops, films, and tapes.

The association also provides a variety of insurance programs, a professional journal and a monthly news magazine, dissemination of information, and promotion of legislation that affects dental hygienists.

The association headquarters are located on the near north side of Chicago.

American Dental Assistants Association

This association was founded in 1925 by Juliette Southard at a meeting in Dallas, Texas. The headquarters office is in Chicago, where all activities are coordinated. The association has held annual meetings since the first one in Texas. This is one of many services offered to members.

Education has been a major concern of the association. In 1940 its education committee provided the first study course outline for dental assistants. During the 1940s, programs were established at vocational, technical, and community schools; today's total is more than 250 such programs.

The association has established a certifying board that requires that dental assistants participate in continuing education to maintain certification. Any assistant who wishes to write the initials C.D.A. after his or her name must be a graduate of an accredited program, pass a written examination, and provide proof of professional ethics. After earning the initial certification, the assistant must obtain at least twelve hours of continuing education each year.

The association is able to offer a variety of insurance plans to its members, provide scholarships, prepare clinics, and offer many opportunities for the exchange of ideas, including a monthly journal.

National Association of Dental Laboratories

In the early 1900s, several dental laboratory groups were formed to establish ethical standards for the industry and to represent the industry in its dealings with members of the dental profession, the dental trade organization, and the federal government.

In 1933, the government ruled that, as an industry, dental laboratories must be operated by a code of fair practices, and a group was organized to formulate these practices.

In 1951, the National Association of Dental Laboratories was formed at a meeting in Chicago. In 1958, the association established the Certified Dental Technician (C.D.T.) program, which is intended to raise the overall performance of the dental laboratory industry and craft and to provide continuing advanced education.

The association works closely with organized dentistry at national and state levels. Its members are encouraged to provide services of a high quality to the dental profession in accordance with state laws.

In 1977, the association established a voluntary national program of certification of dental laboratories in which a framework is set for upgrading laboratory facilities and personnel. Visits are scheduled to the certified laboratories. In the first year, the voluntary program brought in more than a hundred laboratories; many others indicated their support for the program.

There is no national organization for individual laboratory technicians, but those technicians who are part of the C.D.T. program receive several services and benefits: access to group life insurance programs, subscriptions to professional and technical journals, and participation in a variety of study group programs.

There is, however, a professional association for dental laboratories in general, called the National Association of Dental Laboratories. It is located in Virginia and its address is provided in Appendix A.

The aim of these four associations and that of many other organizations within the dental health care field is to provide well-trained professional workers who can offer the best dental care.

Additional Professional Associations

In addition to the American Dental Association, the American Dental Hygienists' Association, the American Dental Assistants Association, and the National Association of Dental Laboratories, there are dozens of other professional associations covering the variety of specialties within dentistry and dental care. Their names, such as Academy for Implants and Transplants or American Academy of Pediatric Dentistry, reveal their focus. Making contact with the organizations that interest you, through a letter, e-mail, or a visit to their website, will provide you with additional career information. A complete list is provided for you in Appendix A.

CHAPTER 2

THE DENTAL TEAM

The concept that a dentist is a person who only repairs teeth is far from correct. The dentist is a scientist who must be dedicated to high standards of health, through prevention, diagnosis, and treatment of all oral diseases and conditions. The dentist maintains the health of not only the teeth but also of all hard and soft tissues in the mouth. The dentist detects oral cancer and other conditions that can harm a patient's total well-being.

The person who combines intelligence, ambition, and social awareness with scientific curiosity can have a rewarding career in dentistry. As a health professional, he or she is highly regarded in the community. The monetary rewards can ensure financial security. However, the greatest reward comes from professional accomplishments.

GENERAL PRACTICE OFFICE

The most common professional setting for dentists, dental hygienists, and dental assistants is in a general practice office. In this setting, a team concept has been established to provide the most efficient care for patients. Team members work in various capacities to provide treatment.

In the general practice office, assistants include a dental hygienist, dental assistant, and sometimes a laboratory technician. Duties of the dental hygienist and the assistant may overlap, but the dental hygienist primarily works independently in caring for the patient, whereas the assistant works directly with the dentist in providing assistance at the chairside.

DENTAL HYGIENIST

The functions performed by the dental hygienist are regulated by state laws; traditionally, the hygienist will:

- collect information about the patient for a medical and dental history
- remove accumulated material from teeth
- expose and process radiographs
- help patients with diet analysis and counseling about nutrition
- instruct patients in correct brushing and cleaning habits
- apply cavity-preventive agents such as sealants and fluoride to teeth
- make impressions of patient's teeth for study models used to evaluate treatment needs
- design and work with dental health programs in schools and communities

Although most hygienists are employed in dental offices, many also work in hospitals, military bases, government agencies, health maintenance organizations, dental schools, research centers, community health services, private industry, and even overseas. The American Dental Hygienists' Association defines dental hygiene as the health profession that "in cooperation with the dental profession, provides services to promote optimal oral health care for the public."

The duties of the hygienist have been expanded in some states to include:

- placing and removing defective restorations and periodontal dressings
- polishing and recontouring defective restorations
- administering local anesthesia
- placing and carving some types of restorations

DENTAL ASSISTANT

The dental assistant, according to the American Dental Assistants Association, "assists with the direct care of patients under the supervision of a dentist."

Assistance may take these forms:

- helping patients feel comfortable before, during, and after dental treatment
- aiding in procedures that are part of dental treatment
- providing diagnostic aids
- sterilizing and disinfecting instruments and equipment
- providing home-care instructions following oral surgical and similar procedures
- preparing instruments and trays for dental procedures
- maintaining records of treatment for patients
- working on programs for control of plaque (a colorless film that forms on teeth)
- assisting in prevention and management of dental and medical emergencies
- setting up and maintaining such office procedures as appointments, payment schedules, infection control regulations, and supply inventories

Employment opportunities for the dental assistant can go beyond the dental office. Assistants may work in any dental specialty offices, in hospitals, in dental schools, or in any federal, state, or community clinic.

DENTAL LABORATORY TECHNICIAN

The laboratory technician is the one person on the dental team who does not deal directly with patients. The technician makes a variety of appliances for the mouth, according to specifications outlined by the dentist. Work involves construction of complete dentures and such small appliances as fixed bridges, removable partial dentures, crowns, inlays, and corrective appliances.

Dental laboratory technicians can work either in a dental office or in a commercial laboratory. In either setting, the technicians' products aid the patients' treatment. Appliances must fit correctly so that the patients look and feel better.

These members of a dental team, working together and using the modern equipment currently available, provide the best health care possible today.

RECEPTIONIST

Although a dental assistant sometimes will perform the duties of a receptionist, often busy dental practices hire one or more people to greet patients, answer the telephone, schedule appointments, file insurance claims, and handle a variety of paperwork and other tasks.

Prior experience in a dental office is not necessarily required; skills acquired as a receptionist in another type of concern could certainly be transferred to a dental practice or related setting. However, someone familiar with the routine of a medical office would certainly have an edge over a competing candidate with unrelated or no experience.

DAILY ROUTINE

For a better understanding of how the dental office team works together, a look at a part of a day's routine in the office of a general practitioner can show how the various participants interact.

A patient is first welcomed into the reception area of the office. If this is a first visit, the patient's dental and appropriate medical history will be taken by the dental assistant. The patient will be introduced to the dental hygienist; the hygienist works in an office that contains a dental chair, the patient's chart, and equipment for cleaning teeth and taking radiographs. All team members follow infection control procedures and wear disposable gloves and masks and protective eyewear.

Radiographs of the patient's teeth are taken and processed by the hygienist, who then performs a complete cleaning (prophylaxis), which includes removing the hardened material (calculus) from all surfaces of the teeth, cleaning with an electric brush, and providing a fluoride treatment. This procedure can also include a description of what is being done and instructions about the best home care for healthy teeth.

After the dental hygienist has finished the cleaning, the patient meets the dentist and chairside assistant. The patient is escorted to one of the several small rooms in the dental operatory; each room has dental chairs and other necessary tools and equipment so that the dentist is able to treat several patients at one time by scheduling different treatments in an overlapping manner. After the dentist examines the patient's entire mouth and looks at the radiographs, the treatment is determined.

While the dentist is performing the examination, the assistant assembles and hands the necessary tools to the dentist. The patient is seated in a comfortable, adjustable chair that can be raised or lowered to allow the dentist and assistant to work conveniently. Instruments and drills are easily accessible.

Treatment for the patient may consist of placement of a restoration (filling) in one or several teeth, construction of a denture to replace missing teeth, or extraction of a tooth that cannot be saved. The dentist also checks for any indications of periodontal (gum) disease, signs of oral cancers, or need for orthodontic (alignment of teeth) or endodontic (root canal) therapy. In all of the procedures, the assistant prepares materials and is ready to hand the dentist the correct tool or instrument.

The laboratory technician prepares the end result of the assistant's and dentist's procedure. The technician follows the design and instructions to construct an individualized crown, bridge, or denture (prosthesis) that fits in the patient's mouth comfortably and matches the color of the patient's teeth.

Several appointments may be necessary to complete the treatment procedure. Each time, the patient is welcomed by the assistant; part of the treatment may be performed by the assistant or hygienist. The prosthesis may be returned to the technician for additional adjustments. The dentist provides the final decision on the success of the treatment, and the patient benefits from the knowledge and expertise of each member of the dental team.

THE DENTAL OFFICE

Before the dental team is assembled and the dental office is in working order, crucial decisions must be made.

After the graduate of a dental school receives a license to practice, the practice and location must be determined. Dentistry is a business, and, in many instances, the dentist has to acquire some business skills in addition to the scientific knowledge he or she must have to set up a practice.

Dentistry is unique in that a dentist must provide physical equipment as well as personal expertise. In contrast, a medical practitioner usually is associated with a hospital and can use the laboratory equipment available there. The dental office must include much of this laboratory equipment, as well as a darkroom, business office, reception room, and individual operatory areas, each one fully equipped.

Office Design

The steps in setting up a dental practice are outlined in *The Successful Dental Practice: An Introduction,* a book prepared by the Council on Dental Practice of the American Dental Association. Several aspects of this book and articles from *The Journal of the American Dental Association* are summarized here to give a picture of how to plan for the establishment of a general practice office. This is the type of office in which the majority of practitioners work with their dental team:

Reception room. This area should be attractive in appearance to welcome patients. It should contain comfortable chairs, reading material, storage for coats, and a device (door chimes) to signal when a patient enters.

Business office. Files, desks, and computers are the equipment needed, with space for appointment books, photocopier, telephones, and other items necessary for scheduling, paying bills, and discussing financial arrangements. This part of the office should be kept separate from the operatories.

Operatories. Two operatories, or one with plans for another, are recommended. For each one, 90 to 100 square feet of space is best. Each operatory will contain a dental chair, cabinet, sink, stools, and equipment area. As in all parts of the office, a pleasant relaxing atmosphere should be created by the use of attractive color schemes.

Laboratory and darkroom. One room can serve both functions unless the dentist plans to have a complete laboratory in which all artificial teeth and other appliances are made. The laboratory should be near the operatories, have adequate plumbing, and include an area for the processing of film. The laboratory should be equipped with products for disinfection and sterilization of the dental office to meet current infection control rec-ommendations. In addition, an area must be set aside for safe disposal of waste materials.

Closets and storage space. Supplies and coats look much better when they can be stored behind closed doors.

Rest room. One rest room is usually sufficient. In some buildings, public rest rooms are provided for staff members and patients.

Optional rooms. For the new practitioner, these areas can be added later to avoid initial expense. For future expansion, these rooms should be considered: private office, staff lounge, conference room, and additional operatories.

Equipment and Services

The office must have many kinds of equipment; used equipment is often available. The advantage of used equipment is the cost, which is one-fourth to one-half the cost of new equipment. However, new equipment requires less maintenance and has a warranty. More modern techniques are part of the design of new equipment, with a wider selection of styles, colors, and functions. An established dental supplier can offer advice on which equipment is best for the budget and style.

A checklist for ordering supplies and setting up services can include the following:

1. Order professional stationery and paper supplies before the office is open.
2. Select appointment forms from dental supply catalogs.
3. Notify utility companies to begin service.
4. Arrange for janitorial services.
5. Set up communication with dental laboratories and dental supply houses.

Location

In choosing a location for the dental office, consider personal preferences:

1. year-round climate
2. other families or persons of similar age and background
3. real estate values
4. spouse's career opportunities
5. recreational and educational facilities
6. cultural, social, and religious affiliations

Professional considerations should include:

1. Can you obtain a license in this area?
2. Would the community accept the type of dentistry you intend to practice?
3. Are other dentists in the area friendly?
4. Are qualified personnel available?
5. Are good dental laboratories accessible?
6. Is there an active local dental society?

These questions can be answered by a chamber of commerce, local dental society, the publications of the American Dental Association, dental supply houses, and financial institutions in the community.

Insurance

Many types of insurance plans—including life, medical, and liability—are available. You must seek advice and compare plans before deciding on the best package for your lifestyle.

CHOOSING EMPLOYEES

At the beginning of your practice, you may hire only one person who will act as receptionist, secretary, and dental assistant. This person must be chosen carefully.

Advertise in the local papers. Use a concise advertisement, and screen applicants by telephone first. Use specific inquiries in conducting the personal interview:

1. Is the applicant's experience, if any, applicable to the needs of the practice?

2. Does the applicant seem flexible? Hours and responsibilities may vary because of emergency situations.
3. Why did the applicant leave a previous position?
4. How is the applicant's health and appearance?
5. Is transportation easily available to the applicant?

In interviewing, use questions that can be answered in detail so you may get to know the applicant. Mention salary and office policies. Write your impressions of the applicant immediately after the interview.

Training Employees

If written records of job descriptions are kept, along with a procedure manual, the office will run more smoothly. Procedures should be outlined for each person on a daily, weekly, monthly, and annual basis.

Employee benefits should be clearly defined: dental care, vacations, sick leave, salary and review, paid holidays, and medical care or pension plan.

Staff meetings should be held regularly to formally discuss problems, allowing feedback from employees to influence changes in office procedures.

Keeping Employees

After the first applicant has been selected, initiate a training period. Have an annual review set up, but, if an employee is not performing adequately, have a review as soon as possible to discuss problems. The staff members, as well as the dentist, are important to the patients' care, so the function of everyone involved contributes to the team-oriented practice.

COMMUNICATING WITH PATIENTS

After the team and facilities are ready for patients, the office atmosphere should generate confidence. Various tools can be used to develop two-way communication.

- Explain the patient's treatment in a positive manner without technical terms. Be sure the patient understands the proposed treatment.
- Emphasize the benefits of treatment. Use radiographs, photographs, or other available visual aids to make a point.
- Ask the dental assistant to help with the explanation, especially with the details of appointment times, length of appointments, and any anesthesia to be given.

Discussion of cases is the foundation of a successful practice. Producing good discussions can bring financial rewards and the satisfaction of good health for patients.

Recall Systems

Regular examinations and professional cleaning are necessary for patients' health. Some type of recall system should be used. It can be a reminder call or postcard. Files should be set up so that each patient can be reminded two or more weeks before the next checkup is scheduled.

Insurance Plans

Many patients now have dental insurance. Office procedures must be established to handle the paperwork involved. The insurance file should be kept separate from the dental file for easy reference.

Discuss the treatment plan and insurance benefits with the patient. After treatment is completed, keep copies of claims and any other items, such as radiographs, that are submitted to the insurance company. These records will be useful if an insurance company loses a claim. Keep records as simple as possible.

Billing Procedures

For patients who do not have dental insurance, payment schedules must be specified. For routine care or minimal treatment, a patient should pay the bill at the time of treatment. This avoids the cost of sending bills and increases the cash flow.

For larger amounts, payment should be made at each visit. Several alternative plans should be offered, depending on the cost and type of treatment.

RECORDKEEPING

Records should be kept for billing, insurance forms, patient reminders, payroll expenses, and income taxes. Systems for keeping all of these types of records are available from dental supply houses. Daily records of all financial activity must be kept; this requires a daily log that includes the list of patients, description of services provided, charges, payments, and balances due. In addition to financial records, an inventory of supplies and equipment must be kept current and accurate.

A record of treatment and other information should be kept with each patient's file. The records should include:

1. personal information, plus insurance coverage
2. medical history with age, weight, height, diseases, medication, allergies, and physician's name
3. diagnosis and treatment plan
4. record of treatment delivered
5. radiographs and photographs
6. patient's financial record of payment

All records should be kept for tax returns: receipts, canceled checks, or any other evidence of financial transactions.

PROFESSIONAL ADVISORS

Because a dentist is trained in dentistry, not business, some aspects of dental practice must be handled by experts from other fields.

Accounting consultant. This person can set up a bookkeeping system and check annual records before income taxes are determined.

Insurance broker. Periodic consultations with a qualified insurance broker can ensure that your insurance needs are met.

Attorney. Tax advice, leasing contracts, and partnerships can be handled by an attorney.

Investment counselor. Many types of investments can be made and an experienced counselor can provide seasoned judgment and guidance.

QUALITY OF CARE

After all the preparation is made, the ultimate basis for a successful practice is your professional reputation and concern for patients. You will need to educate patients in oral health, communicate with them about their treatment, convey a sense of confidence in yourself and your practice, follow through with your concern, and, most important, provide the highest quality of care.

CHAPTER 3

SPECIALTIES IN DENTISTRY

Nearly 90 percent of dentists are in private practice, working alone or with one or more partners. About 80 percent of all dentists practice general dentistry; the other 20 percent are in one of the eight specialties that dentists may choose to study.

The eight special areas are dental public health, endodontics, oral pathology, oral and maxillofacial surgery, orthodontics, pediatric dentistry, periodontics, and prosthodontics. All of these specialties require some additional training beyond a degree in dentistry.

DENTAL PUBLIC HEALTH

A career in public health dentistry offers a chance to serve a community rather than an individual patient. The responsibility of this career is preventive dentistry on a large scale. There are many opportunities for research and teaching.

People in the public health service are concerned with controlling dental diseases and promoting dental health through organized efforts. They may work on such projects as rehabilitation of patients with mouth deformities, study of the effects of fluoridation on schoolchildren, or research on methods to decrease tooth decay. The results of the research are often applied in organized community studies. The public health dentists may use the newest research tools such as electron microscopes to conduct their studies. In many instances, they work in federal government laboratories, and the results of their research and study are distributed by the government. Dental education of the public is a chief concern of dentists in this branch of dentistry.

ENDODONTICS

This fairly new specialty of dentistry deals with the treatment of the pulp of a tooth. This treatment can mean the difference between saving or extracting a tooth. The procedure involves careful, sterile treatment of the roots of the teeth. Each tooth has one or more roots at its base, and each root has one or more canals in its center. Within each canal is a small opening so that the blood vessels and nerves of the pulp can connect with similar structures in the bone surrounding the root end.

If the pulp tissue is injured (by an accident or blow to the teeth) or decay has reached the tissue, the pulp tissue must be removed and the area filled with a sterile material. The endodontist performing this procedure deals with the inside dimensions of the tooth. The inside of the root canals cannot be viewed directly, so the endodontist must make exact measurements with fine instruments that clean and file the root canals and then check the measurements with radiographs. Manual dexterity is required to perform these procedures.

The endodontist must have a knowledge of the biology of the pulp as well as the anatomy of the teeth and jaws. This specialist must learn a great deal about oral pathology (study of diseases) and bacteriology (study of microscopic plants that can cause diseases).

ORAL PATHOLOGY

Oral pathology deals with the nature of diseases that affect the mouth and areas around the mouth. These specialists work primarily in a laboratory, although they may also have office practices. They may teach or do research for a college or for a part of the military services.

Oral pathologists must understand diseases of the mouth and also must have a thorough understanding of the entire human body. For example, tumors of the mouth are studied by oral pathologists. Treatment for many types of tumors is radiation. The oral pathologist must be aware of the effects of radiation not only on the mouth and the tumor but also on the rest of the body.

People who choose this part of dentistry must be interested in extensive research and use of such laboratory procedures as clinical, microscopic, radiographic, and biochemical examinations.

ORAL AND MAXILLOFACIAL SURGERY

In this part of dentistry, people must be "on call" for emergencies. The oral surgeon is often affiliated with a university or hospital or both. Many patients may have been in accidents or have problems that require immediate attention: These problems do not always occur during regular office hours.

Oral surgeons do not fill cavities or make dentures; instead they extract teeth, treat injuries and infections, and perform any necessary surgery. They repair defects of the mouth, either those that appear at birth or those caused by an accident. They can align parts of the structure of the mouth, the upper jaw (maxilla), or the lower jaw (mandible). They can remove tumors. A complete knowledge of the use of anesthesia is a necessity for this type of dentistry.

Those considering this dental specialty must be prepared for several years of graduate study after they receive their degrees in general dentistry. They must pass several examinations: oral and written tests, plus a clinical test in which the actual diagnosis and treatment of patients are required.

ORTHODONTICS

This branch of dentistry is concerned with the correction of irregularities of teeth to provide normal occlusion (coming together of teeth in the mouth), plus a pleasing appearance. Correction of these irregularities can help appearance, chewing ability, and speech habits. Most orthodontic patients are children, but currently many adults are also having this correction made.

Orthodontists are responsible for making models or casts of the patient's mouth to show how the irregular teeth can be corrected. To make the corrections, fixed appliances (braces) are placed in the patient's mouth. Treatment can last from two to four years. The patient makes weekly visits at first, then monthly appointments. The appliances, which are adjusted by the orthodontist, move the teeth gradually into a better arrangement. The final results offer correct position of teeth, normal use of the muscles of the mouth, and better general health.

Orthodontists work in private offices, alone or with partners, meeting patients on a regular basis. Treatments go on for such long periods that the orthodontist must be able to encourage patients about the final results. An ability to diagnose a patient's condition and to have a great deal of patience are important to someone in this field of dentistry.

PEDIATRIC DENTISTRY

These dentists take care of children and teach them how to care for their teeth. Pediatric dentists must understand the processes of how the child's mouth develops. Because the primary (baby) set of teeth is important to the correct development of the permanent teeth, they must be cared for and treated when problems arise.

Children must be carefully taught the importance of caring for their teeth so that good oral hygiene habits can be instilled early; this is an important part of the pediatric dentist's job. The dentist must overcome any fears a child may have of the dental office or the instruments used; a background in child psychology is necessary for this type of dentistry.

Dental treatment of children must be painless and quick; it is difficult for children to remain quiet very long, so long-term treatment is difficult. Understanding children's capabilities and habits will help the dentist work successfully. Also, as problems in children's mouths are usually minor, treatment can be swift. The young tissue of children's mouths heals rapidly, and this, too, is an advantage.

Pediatric dentists also treat special patients—those who are mentally, emotionally, or physically handicapped and have special requirements to keep their teeth healthy. These patients use different types of equipment to help them brush and clean teeth, and the dentist must instruct patients in their use. Much patience and understanding is required from those planning a career in pediatric dentistry.

PERIODONTICS

The supporting tissues of the teeth are called gums or, scientifically, the gingiva of the mouth. If this gingiva is destroyed, teeth are lost. This destruction is caused by several factors: poor occlusion, food impaction, incorrect or inadequate restoration of teeth, irritants of several types, or a disease that affects other parts of the body as well as teeth. As the gingiva becomes infected, bacteria can enter and destroy this tissue. Specialists in periodontics must diagnose and stop this destructive process.

Periodontists work almost entirely with adult patients. The cause of the loss of gingiva can be complex, so that knowledge of the disease process is required. If the patient has a disease that affects other parts of the body, the periodontist must work with a laboratory and other means of diagnosis to determine the exact cause and cure. Surgery is often performed in which part of the infected gingiva is removed.

Preventive treatment is usually the most effective method of control. Periodontists must perform thorough cleaning of a patient's teeth and gums and instruct the patient in correct cleaning processes to prevent recurrence of the disease.

PROSTHODONTICS

This part of dentistry is concerned with the replacement of teeth that have been lost because of disease or accidents. Replacement can be of a single tooth or all of the teeth in the mouth. A prosthodontist can also reconstruct parts of the jaws with artificial substitutes.

Dentists may practice general dentistry along with performing prosthodontic treatment. However, patients who have problems with their replacement teeth may consult a prosthodontic specialist for correction of their problems. The specialist must be skilled in all the new processes of restoration so that the replacement teeth not only fit properly but also enhance the patient's appearance. The dentist is helped by the dental laboratory technician to construct the correct replacements for teeth.

Patients who consult prosthodontists may have teeth so badly deformed or diseased that the teeth may all have to be extracted. The specialist must then reconstruct the entire mouth of the patient with complete dentures or with implants, providing teeth that fit and perform correctly and give a pleasing appearance. Much skill, time, and effort are required to achieve this finished effect.

GENERAL PRACTITIONER

These eight specialties require various degrees of advanced preparation and education. However, the general practitioner with a dental degree can and does perform many or all parts of these special duties in the everyday office routine. The general practitioner deals with children and adults, extracts and restores teeth, examines tissues for disease, and instructs patients in the care of their teeth.

The general practitioners are knowledgeable in many of the special areas and, in most instances, know when a specialist must be consulted—when a patient's condition requires additional treatment beyond the scope of the practitioner. A spirit of cooperation distinguishes those in the dental care field to ensure the best possible treatment for patients.

In all of the foregoing areas of practice, the dentist acts as the leader of a group whose aim is to achieve dental health. Each dentist is helped in this endeavor by the hygienist, assistant, and technician.

FEDERAL DENTAL SERVICES

Many opportunities for the practice of any type of dentistry can be found in the armed forces of the United States where there is always a demand for skilled dentists. In addition, those who have been awarded grants from the Health Education Assistance Loan Program will not be required to repay their loans while they are serving in the armed forces.

Dentists who enter the armed forces are commissioned as captains in the army and the air force and as lieutenants in the navy. Graduates of dental schools are also eligible for federal civil service positions and for commissions (equivalent to naval lieutenants) in the United States Public Health Service.

PUBLIC SERVICE CAREERS

After completing the necessary training or education, a dentist, hygienist, assistant, or laboratory technician can use these skills in many situations to provide service to the public.

This public service can include the Peace Corps, with service inside or outside the United States being possible. Inside the United States, the geographic area may be one in which there are not enough dentists or other dental employees to provide service to a given population. An example is the work done by the Indian Health Service by dental teams working in remote parts of the United States to offer treatment to native Americans living on reservations.

In addition, federal hospitals, prisons, and other, often remote facilities need to be served. Scholarships are available to those who volunteer to serve in these understaffed areas after they complete their training and education.

Many religious and charitable organizations maintain missionary dentists and assistants in remote areas of the United States and in other countries. The national organizations of Protestant and Catholic churches are responsible for staffing a large number of medical and dental missions. Knowledge of a foreign language can be a requirement for this work in an overseas assignment.

THE ROLE OF DENTAL RESEARCH

Additional support for the work of the dental health care practitioner is offered by those involved in dental research. Research can involve high school students in a science fair, dental school students in competition for a place at a national scientific session, or professional scientists in search of answers about the cause of caries (decay). Contributions to the body of dental care knowledge are continually being made.

The history of dentistry shows how the development of the microscope and the discovery and use of radiographs were crucial to the progress of dental care. In the same way, the advances made in research today in improved materials, procedures, and instruments add to the efficiency and performance of those who care for patients. Experimentation and discovery have resulted in many improvements in dental treatment.

Many pioneers in research have contributed to these improvements. An outstanding person in American dentistry was investigator and teacher Greene V. Black of Illinois. If Pierre Fauchard is the founder of dentistry, then G. V. Black is the founder of modern American clinical dentistry.

Dr. Black was born in 1836 and died in 1915. During his lifetime, several dental journals were started, dental schools were founded, and dental societies were formed. His influence was felt in all of these areas, and especially in research.

Dr. Black did not attend a formal dental school but received his training through an apprenticeship; his ability to observe and study compensated for whatever lack of formal education he may have had.

He was a practitioner in Jacksonville, Illinois, for fourteen years. In addition to his practice, he also lectured on pathology at Missouri Dental College two days a week, contributed articles to dental journals, and served as an officer in dental societies. He studied histology, chemistry, metallurgy, pathology, and dental processes. He educated himself in several of these fields by making microscopic slides of tissue. Visits to workers in fine metal—jewelers and clock makers—taught him how better to handle metals in the practice of dentistry. He invented a cord-driven, foot-powered dental engine and set up a shop for the manufacture and sale of these machines. He studied foreign languages in order to read the works of Lister, Pasteur, and others in the original versions. In 1878, he was awarded a Doctor of Dental Surgery degree by Missouri Dental College after he had lectured in the school for eight years.

In 1897, Dr. Black became dean of Northwestern University Dental School, Chicago, then one of the largest and most influential dental schools in the world. He continued to publish the results of his studies and experiments. His work in practical dentistry, *Operative Dentistry,* was published in 1908 in two volumes. These books combined his knowledge of basic dental science with his procedures in clinical dentistry. His conclusions after many years of research in dental decay, filling materials, antiseptics, dental instruments, and many other topics are still honored and studied today.

Not all researchers and investigators have had the same impact in as many areas of dentistry as did G. V. Black, but other contributions have been valuable in establishing dental science. W. D. Miller of Ohio studied bacteriology and published results of his research to show that microorganisms are the cause of tooth decay. His book, *The Microorganisms of the Mouth,* was published in 1889.

Other more contemporary researchers have included Dr. H. Trendley Dean, who investigated the benefits of fluoride; Dr. Robert Nelsen and his associates, who developed the high-speed dental handpiece; and Dr. Ray Bowen, who pioneered the use of new composite resins used for restorations of teeth.

Currently, researchers are developing new technological methods for more efficient patient care: use of lasers in surgery, implants to replace damaged bone, and computerized X-rays.

National Programs

National research programs were sponsored by the American Dental Association as early as 1908. The Council on Dental Research of the American Dental Association has two programs, one started in 1928 at the National Bureau of Standards in Washington, DC, and the other in 1941 at the National Institute of Dental Research in Bethesda, Maryland. The program at the National Bureau of Standards focuses on dental materials and their aspects, and the work at the National Institute of Dental Research concentrates on research in biological sciences. In addition, research projects are carried out at the laboratories in the headquarters building of the American Dental Association in Chicago.

One of the biggest factors in this field was the establishment by twenty-five members of the International Association for Dental Research in 1920. This group publishes *The Journal of Dental Research* and has established annual meetings at which papers representing the most current findings are given. The association has grown to include international divisions at which more than a thousand research papers can be given during a three- to four-day schedule.

Foundations and philanthropists have contributed to dental research through establishment of such programs as the Gies Foundation; the Eastman Dental Center, Rochester, New York; and the Zoller Memorial Clinic at the University of Chicago. Nearly all dental schools and colleges conduct continuing research programs.

During the 1940s, the government entered the field of dental research when the navy asked the National Research Council for advice on military dental standards. A dental advisory committee was formed to offer aid and approve grants. The Veterans Administration (now the Department of Veterans Affairs), the army, and air force began their own research programs.

In 1948, the National Institute of Dental Research was established. Funds were made available for research projects and fellowships for study at various dental institutions. The program at the National Institute provides training for those who are interested in basic sciences and helps other dental institutions set up research projects. As part of the National Institutes of Health, the National Institute of Dental Research has its own building in Bethesda, Maryland, constructed in the 1960s.

The National Institute of Dental Research involves many disciplines in the search for answers to problems that affect the mouth. For example, an investigation into the cause of caries can involve biochemists, nutritionists, geneticists, pathologists, and other scientists. Use of sophisticated and complex aids such as the scanning electron microscope and computerized equipment has aided research methods.

The institute encourages each dental school to offer summer research awards to students. A dental student, hygienist, or assistant can complete a research project and report on it at a meeting of the American Association for Dental Research or the International Association for Dental Research. There are many awards for outstanding research today.

Clinical Research

Clinical, or applied, research is being done to correct dental problems. An example is the help given to infants born with a cleft, or split, upper lip. Corrective surgery and therapy for each infant can cost as much as $20,000. If this condition can be avoided, much money can be saved, but of greater importance is solving the problems inflicted on a newborn child who cannot eat or drink because of the split upper lip. Research is being done to determine when, in the development of the unborn child, the mouth is not completely formed. Investigation is also being done to find the best method of surgical repair for this condition, as well as the best way to teach a child to speak after the defect has been repaired. This is one of many ways in which dental research is helping patients have happier lives through clinical application of research findings.

Current topics being studied by research teams include temporomandibular joint dysfunction, reduction of dental anxiety, and the human immunodeficiency virus that causes AIDS.

Research training is offered at nearly all dental schools as well as other institutions. Schools are equipped to offer students the chance to become familiar with the techniques, discipline, and procedures necessary to conduct scientific research. Training is offered at both the undergraduate and graduate level.

Another source of research programs is the manufacturers of dental materials and equipment. Companies that produce toothpastes perform ongoing research in an attempt to improve their products. Companies that produce the materials used in dental fillings do controlled tests on these materials to check their long-term retention in teeth, their compatibility with tooth enamel, and their deterioration in the mouth. Gold was once used extensively as a filling material, but as the price soared, manufacturers were forced to investigate new materials as a replacement. Also, as more practitioners treat handicapped patients, new equipment must be devised to help these patients sit easily in a dental chair (rather than their wheelchair) and to offer them specially designed toothbrushes to help them care for their teeth.

Dental research provides support and essential background for practitioners in all of the dentistry disciplines. It is an area where workers interested in scientific methods and application of these methods can find employment. The ultimate benefit of research is to the dental patients, who are cared for by dental practitioners aware of and working with the latest advances.

SALARIES FOR DENTISTS

According to the American Dental Association, earnings for dentists with a private general dentistry practice average between $120,000 to $150,000 a year on up. Dentists with a specialty practice generally earn more, averaging between $175,000 to $250,000 a year or more.

Dentists in the beginning years of their practice often earn less. They have school loans to pay off and the expense of setting up a new office. Those established in midcareers earn more.

A relatively large proportion of dentists are self-employed. Like other business owners, these dentists must provide their own health insurance, life insurance, retirement benefits, and must also pay salaries to dental assistants, hygienists, and other staff members.

CHAPTER 4

AREAS OF SERVICE

The range of opportunities for dental hygienists, dental assistants, and laboratory technicians is increasing as their responsibilities expand. In addition to work in a dentist's office or in a laboratory, there are other fields of service.

DENTAL HYGIENISTS

Dental hygienists hold about 150,000 jobs throughout the United States and Canada. Because multiple job holding is common in this field, the number of jobs greatly exceeds the number of hygienists.

More than half of all dental hygienists work part-time—less than thirty-five hours a week. Almost all dental hygienists work in private dental offices. The remainder work in public health agencies, hospitals, school systems, industrial plants, dental hygiene schools, clinics, and for state and federal government agencies. Some work overseas.

Employment of dental hygienists is expected to grow much faster than the average for all occupations through the year 2006, in response to increasing demand for dental care and the greater substitution of hygienists for services previously performed by dentists. Job prospects are expected to remain very good, unless the number of dental hygienist program graduates grows much faster than during the last decade, resulting in a much larger pool of qualified applicants.

Demand will be stimulated by population growth and greater retention of natural teeth by the larger number of middle-aged and elderly people.

Also, dentists are likely to employ more hygienists for several reasons. As dentists' workloads increase, they are expected to hire more hygienists to perform preventive dental care such as cleaning, so they may devote their own time to more profitable procedures.

Older dentists, who are less likely to employ dental hygienists, will leave and be replaced by recent graduates, who are more likely to do so.

In a general practice office, the hygienist is usually part of a team with the dentist, assistant, and technician. In this setting, the hygienist works with patients of all ages and types of conditions. The hygienist learns to cope with children who come for their first appointments, with people of every age who have neglected care of their teeth, with elderly patients who need advice about caring for dentures, and with many others. The treatment of these patients includes instructing them about care of their teeth and gums.

With the current concern about acquired immune deficiency syndrome (AIDS) and other infectious diseases, dental team members today must practice infection control measures. Hygienists are often responsible for many disinfectant procedures. Each team member must wear disposable gloves, masks, and protective eyewear when working with patients.

In an office in which special oral conditions are treated, the hygienist must acquire additional knowledge about these conditions. For example, if the dentist is a pediatric dentist, the hygienist should have advanced training in child psychology to be able to teach children about the care of their teeth, to give them nutritional advice, and to make their experience in a dental office as pleasant as possible.

In orthodontic practice, hygienists see the patients for long periods, as the corrective movement of teeth is a gradual process. Hygienists prepare full-mouth X-rays, make impressions for study casts, and perform cleaning and fluoride treatments. The hygienist also gives complete instructions about home care and eating habits when correctional appliances are worn.

For the positions just described, a two-year educational program usually offers sufficient training. However, if an administrative or independent position is your goal, a bachelor's degree from a four-year program is required; in some instances, an M.P.H. (Master of Public Health) is a further requirement.

Public Health Service

For people with M.P.H. degrees, and for some dental hygienists without the degree, public health service employment is available. Each state has a department of public health, and many employ dental hygienists for community health education and administrative work. This work can be as varied as lecturing on fluoridation of water, preparing pamphlets and films for distribution in schools, and conducting training sessions for elementary schoolteachers. Hygienists may be employed by a school system both to work directly with schoolchildren and to train those who do.

Some hygienists work in hospitals as part of a dental program. Others treat handicapped patients in hospitals and other institutions. In these situations, the hygienist serves the physically handicapped for whom special cleaning aids might be devised, for example, specially bent or longer handles on toothbrushes or electric toothbrushes mounted on brackets. For mentally handicapped persons, the hygienist must find methods to encourage and reinforce these patients in the care of their teeth.

With nearly two hundred schools offering training programs for dental hygienists, there is a need for teachers. Teaching duties depend on the specialty of the hygienist and usually include supervision of students as they learn to work with patients in actual clinical settings.

Working Abroad

Chances to work abroad are also available for the dental hygienist. In some European countries, dental hygiene is currently just becoming accepted as a profession. In Great Britain, however, the dental hygienist has been working independently since 1957. In New Zealand, dental nurses provide all dental care for children up to age twelve. Duties of the profession can change from country to country, so a study of each one and its language should be part of any decision to work abroad.

From the descriptions of careers in dental hygiene, you can see that hours and working conditions do not always ensure a forty-hour work week. Hours can be spent in a nine to five routine, perhaps four and a half weekdays, plus a half-day on Saturdays. Traveling from one school to another can be part of the schedule for a school employee. Hours in the classroom and preparing for lectures can add up to more than a forty-hour week for an educator. However, it is a career that can be adjusted to many lifestyles. The hygienist can work part-time and so have time for a young family, or share a job with another hygienist to allow both of them to keep up their clinical skills. The options are many.

Salaries for Dental Hygienists

Of all the dental technicians—dental assistants, dental laboratory technicians/ceramists—dental hygienists generally command the highest salaries. Earnings of dental hygienists are affected by geographic location, employment setting, and education and experience. Dental hygienists who work in private dental offices may be paid on an hourly, daily, salary, or commission basis.

According to the American Dental Association, experienced dental hygienists who work thirty-two hours a week or more in a private practice averaged about $900 a week. Benefits vary substantially by practice setting and may be contingent upon full-time employment.

Dental hygienists who work for school systems, public health agencies, the federal government, or state agencies usually have substantial benefits. Dental hygienists who work overseas may also be provided with additional perks such as free transportation, housing allowances, and longer paid vacations.

DENTAL ASSISTANTS

Approximately 180,000 people work full- or part-time as dental assistants in North America. Most assistants work in private dental offices for dentists who practice individually or in a group practice.

The job outlook for dental assistants is as good as that for dental hygienists. Jobs for dental assistants are expected to grow at an equally fast rate in response to increasing demand for dental care.

The work of an assistant in a general practice office depends on the size and nature of the practice. The assistant may be the only employee in a small practice. In those conditions, the assistant may answer the telephone, do the billing, schedule appointments, and help the dentist at chairside.

In a large practice, these duties are divided among several assistants. One may be the office manager who handles all records, schedules appointments, orders supplies, and is in charge of all business functions. Another assistant (or two) would work directly at the chairside with the dentist and handle all instruments. In some offices, duties overlap, and assistants may be able to fill in at each other's jobs during lunch hours and vacations. In a busy office with one or more dentists, the ratio of assistants to dentists may be as high as five to one.

In the offices of dental specialists, duties of an assistant depend on the nature of the speciality. In orthodontic and pediatric practice, the assistant must be able to work well with children and teenagers. In helping to provide endodontic and oral surgery treatment, the assistant's role resembles that of a surgical nurse, as sterile conditions must be maintained. If the assistant is working with an oral pathologist, knowledge of microscopic, biochemical, or other laboratory examinations is necessary.

Hospital Settings

Dental assistants may also choose to practice in hospital settings: clinics and armed forces bases, university and industrial facilities, institutions for the handicapped, and government-operated hospitals. In short, any place dentistry is practiced in some form, an assistant is needed.

The choice of this career is not always a final one. The assistant may return to school to acquire additional skills and qualifications necessary to practice as a hygienist or dentist. Also, teachers are needed in the more than 250 training programs for dental assistants. Experience plus additional course work can lead to a career in education.

No matter what part of the assistant's career is most appealing, you should be sure that you enjoy people and are able to make them comfortable in a sometimes tense situation. Because the assistant is often the first person to deal with the patient both in person and on the telephone, the initial impression is important. The way in which the assistant is able to relate to the patient may mean the difference between a pleased or dissatisfied patient.

Salaries for Dental Assistants

According to the American Dental Association, dental assistants who work thirty-two hours a week or more average more than $400 a week. Hourly earnings run $11 on average.

DENTAL LABORATORY TECHNICIANS/ DENTAL CERAMISTS

Dental laboratory technicians are like pharmacists; they fill prescriptions, but their prescriptions come from dentists and are for crowns, bridges, dentures, and other dental devices.

They work with plaster, wax, and porcelain with small handheld tools through a variety of the stages required to produce the device. In some laboratories dental laboratory technicians perform all stages of the work; in other labs the different stages are assigned to different technicians.

Technicians also may specialize in one of five areas: orthodontic appliances, crown and bridge, complete dentures, partial dentures, or ceramics.

Technicians who make porcelain and acrylic restorations are called dental ceramists.

Dental laboratory technicians hold about fifty-five thousand jobs throughout North America. Most jobs are in commercial dental laboratories, which usually are small, privately owned businesses with fewer than five employees. However, some laboratories are larger; a few employ more than two hundred technicians.

Approximately one technician in seven is self-employed, a higher proportion than in most other occupations.

Dental laboratories are located chiefly in large cities and states with large populations. Many laboratories fill orders for dentists who work far away and have no laboratory nearby. All work is done by following written instructions from dentists and using impressions of the patient's mouth made by the dentist.

About a thousand dental laboratory technicians work in dentists' offices. For these technicians, written instruction is still given, but a problem in fitting or changing a denture or appliance can be solved while the patient is in the office.

Other employment opportunities are in hospitals that provide dental services and in government agencies such as the military services and Department of Veterans Affairs hospitals and clinics. In addition, firms that manufacture dental equipment often hire technicians as technical or sales representatives. These manufacturing firms also employ technicians for research in new types of materials and equipment.

The fifty-plus accredited programs for training dental laboratory technicians also offer opportunities for teaching. Usually experience, rather than a degree, is the most useful factor in becoming an educator in this field.

No matter where the technician's job is geographically located, the environment is a laboratory setting. Technicians have their own area in which to work. This area would include an individual workbench with gas burners, grinding and polishing machines, and various hand tools.

Trainees usually learn to work first in plaster and graduate to more difficult materials. Some technicians specialize in one phase of work; others perform the full range—from making crowns and dentures (removable and fixed), through corrective appliances. Many materials are used: plastic, silver, stainless steel, porcelain, and composite resins. New materials are being tried and tested for various appliances and prostheses.

If you plan to follow a career as a dental laboratory technician, you need manual skill, ability to work with small devices and appliances, and attentiveness to detail.

Salaries for Dental Laboratory Technicians/Dental Ceramists

Data are limited, but past surveys show that in general wages for dental laboratory technicians/dental ceramists are much less than those for hygienists and assistants. Hourly earnings have been reported as low as minimum wage for trainees, moving upward to approximately $15 to $20 an hour for more experienced workers.

DENTAL-RELATED CAREERS

Dental Sales and Manufacture

Other opportunities exist in dental-related positions. Many manufacturers supply business forms, office furniture, dental chairs and attachments, laboratory equipment, instruments and accessories, restorative materials, and radiographic equipment.

Sellers and manufacturers of the specialized equipment must have a knowledge of dental procedures to produce, understand, and explain their products. Persons who are qualified in one type of dentistry, especially dental laboratory technicians, may move to the area of dental equipment, such as in manufacturing or sales.

Jobs with Dental Organizations

Nearly all state and regional dental societies have an executive director and staffs that vary in size depending on the size of the society. Most of the directors and staff members do not have degrees in dentistry, but they do have some dental background or experience.

Many national organizations related to a dental specialty have their own offices, for example, the Association of Oral and Maxillofacial Surgeons, the American Association of Oral and Maxillofacial Surgeons, the American Academy of Pediatric Dentistry, the American College of Prosthodontists, the American Academy of Periodontology, and many others. In addition to their other work, each group produces a professional journal related to their specialty. Dental writing and editing are associated careers.

Research

Persons who are interested in scientific research can find a career in developing new materials and methods to be used for better treatment of teeth. They can be employed by research institutions or by manufacturers who are interested in developing better toothbrushes, toothpastes, or other aids for better oral health.

Education

Community colleges, universities, and graduate schools involved in dental education need teachers and administrators who are interested in sharing their knowledge with others. Educators can also find governmental employment in health care education programs that concentrate on providing information to the public through newspaper, radio, and television.

EXPANDED DUTIES

The dental team concept described in Chapter 2 is the traditional one in which the dentist, assistant, hygienist, and sometimes the technician, work together in one office. However, the work of the dental hygienist is becoming more specialized and, in some instances, more independent.

The responsibility of the dental hygienist has become one in which more knowledge and training have led to increased duties and additional functions. The dental hygienist has functioned primarily in the realm of preventive procedures and direct patient education. The original concept of the dental hygienist, as envisioned by Dr. Alfred Fones in the early 1900s, was that of a person responsible for preventive dentistry. As approximately 90 percent of the United States population is affected by some form of dental disease or problem, the need for preventive dentistry is extensive, and services of the dental hygienist are in demand.

Although nearly all hygienists working today are employed in a dental office, some opportunities exist for the hygienist to work in alternate settings. Supervision must meet standards set by state laws.

The term *general supervision* has been interpreted to mean supervision of dental procedures based on the authorization given by a licensed dentist, but not requiring the physical presence of the supervising dentist during the performance of some procedures, for example:

1. oral prophylaxis
2. applying topical fluoride to teeth
3. root planing
4. polishing and contouring restorations
5. oral exfoliative cytology
6. applying pit and fissure sealants
7. preliminary examinations including but not limited to: periodontal charting; intraoral and extraoral examination of soft tissue; charting of lesions, restorations, and missing teeth; classifying occlusion; myofunctional evaluation

A general supervision requirement may be met when the dentist writes the prescription for a cleaning for a patient or does the examination to diagnose a cleaning. The treatment facility in which a hygienist works may be under the jurisdiction and control of a supervising licensed dentist. Many hygienists work as independent contractors, in a business agreement between the hygienist and dentist. Some states allow expanded duties—and even independent practice—for hygienists.

Increased Responsibilities

Having the hygienist handle additional treatment procedures has been economically feasible, as the dentist is then free to provide the more complicated procedures that are needed for the patient. The increased duties provide a challenge for those who plan to enter this profession.

The dental hygienist, working in any setting, is often the first person to see a patient and frequently is the one who remains in closest contact with the patient in follow-up care and treatment. The hygienist's concern for preventing dental disease is evident in the way the hygienist instructs patients.

The goals of the total treatment plan are to:

1. eliminate the disease and restore the patient's mouth to its normal function and
2. counsel the patient in self-care procedures and give follow-up professional care to prevent recurrence of the disease.

At the first interview with the patient, several objectives should be accomplished:

1. The patient's history should be completed. Previous treatment of dental problems, any major health concerns, and specific medications the patient is taking must be included. The patient's nutritional health and emotional stability can be evaluated. In the history interview process, the skillful hygienist can establish a rapport with the patient, which can aid patients in communicating their needs and concerns.
2. The oral examination of the patient is made, and the findings are recorded. The hygienist must be gentle but firm and note oral cleanliness, look for any problems, and take radiographs when required.
3. Cleaning the teeth may be the most valuable of all tasks, as the hygienist can instruct while the cleaning takes place. Individualized instruction becomes very important in the first and follow-up visits. The hygienist must emphasize, in many ways, depending on the age and experience of the patient, the importance of brushing and cleaning the teeth.

Education of Patients

In this educational process, the hygienist must emphasize rules for good dental health:

1. brush and floss thoroughly at least once a day
2. brush after meals when possible
3. cut down on the amount of foods that contain sugar, and avoid sweet snacks between meals
4. use a fluoride daily
5. have regular professional checkups and cleaning

The hygienist can demonstrate correct brushing and flossing techniques, using methods suitable for each age group. In dealing with children, the hygienist must be careful to explain the activity in terms the child can understand. Special problems, such as removing material from beneath braces or other oral devices, must be solved.

In a pediatric practice, the hygienist should be aware of what type of activity or explanation appeals to each age group. For example, a three-year-old child who may be making a first visit to the office usually has a friendly attitude and a desire to talk, making it difficult to have the child remain quiet long enough to perform a satisfactory examination. The hygienist can use a positive, friendly approach and simple language with little explanation. Sometimes a prop, such as a puppet, can be useful.

Four- and five-year-old children can be quite cooperative and begin to understand the process and importance of cleaning teeth. Often, a child this age can be so eager to please and so impressed with the importance of toothbrushing that he or she will not go to bed without brushing. Children can help in the procedures and are proud of their accomplishments.

A six-year-old child may be having to move from close family ties for the first time and may resent any additional intrusion. If too much stress is placed on a child whose behavior is already a problem, the dental experience may not be a happy one. In some instances, it is best to postpone treatment.

Until the age of twelve, when the child patient is "almost an adult," the growing-up process may offer problems not related to the dental office but may cause the child to resent treatment. Special patience and understanding are required to meet not only children's dental needs but also their emotional needs. The hygienist must learn to recognize these situations and be able to cope with them.

Teaching Program

With patients of any age, an effective teaching program provides both detailed information and principles to guide and motivate the patient. With the hygienist's concern and professional enthusiasm, patients can be motivated to cooperate. Several basic steps can be used:

1. Demonstration. The patient should be taught to hold the brush and the correct methods of brushing and flossing.
2. Evaluation. A disclosing tablet that stains the teeth in areas where cleaning is incomplete can be used to show the patient how well he or she has brushed.

3. Practice. During the second or third visit, the patient should be able to show how well brushing has been practiced at home.
4. Results. The patient's progress should be recorded, and the hygienist should point out the improvement, or lack of it, and discuss in an encouraging manner how to solve any problems.

Instruction in nutrition should be given by the hygienist. Foods to be avoided should be listed, as well as those that are the most helpful. Keeping a food diary in which a patient lists all the foods he or she eats can give the patient a chance to study dietary habits. This diary can be reviewed with the hygienist.

Emergency Care

Additionally, the dental hygienist is sometimes responsible for dealing with emergencies that can occur in the office. Emergency care through first aid measures is performed rarely, but the individual trained in a health care profession must be able to react correctly.

The first step is, of course, to understand the patient's needs well enough so that emergencies can be prevented. If an adequate history has been taken, the hygienist will be aware of any special physical conditions that could require first aid. The hygienist will also have information concerning allergies or drug reactions, or any disease for which the patient is under the care of a physician and the type of treatment.

Types of emergencies that can occur include prolonged bleeding, difficulty in breathing, shock, heart failure, seizures, or fainting. The first aid procedures for each of these conditions should be reviewed regularly by the hygienist. Knowing the technique for cardiopulmonary resuscitation and artificial respiration can be invaluable in a crisis situation. Training for resuscitation is a requirement for licensure in some states. The office first aid kit should be updated regularly and kept in a convenient location.

Other Procedures

Oral surgery procedures require the use of anesthesia, and hygienists, because of their formal education and training, can be a part of this health care delivery system. The hygienist can be involved in various phases of anesthesia administration, from the preparation of the drug for the dentist to the actual administration of the drug, if permitted by state law.

It is often the hygienist's responsibility to monitor the patient for the duration of the drug's effect so that the drug's actions, including side effects, will be known. The hygienist can prepare the patient for the surgical procedure and for follow-up care when nutritional intake is limited by the oral surgery procedure.

In addition to responsibility during oral surgery procedures, the hygienist can be the clinician or advisor before, during, and after treatment of periodontal (gum) disease by the periodontist. The hygienist can also aid the orthodontist by teaching patients how to care for teeth while braces are worn. To be helpful in more detailed treatment, the hygienist must have a reasonable working knowledge of malocclusion (a problem with the way teeth come together), its cause, and treatment.

In other dental specialties, the more knowledge attained by the hygienist, the greater is the responsibility acquired.

Special Patients

Dealing with patients with special needs means extra time and effort expended by the hygienist. Mentally handicapped patients often have fears and anxieties and are easily discouraged; however, their dental care is vital, as their handicaps are great enough without adding oral problems to their lives. So, if the hygienist can prepare the patient carefully, repeat instructions many times, and provide adequate brushing devices, the patient's problems can be lessened at least a little.

Patients in hospitals for long-term stays need the help and encouragement of a dental hygienist. The hygienist may be the first to observe the beginning of a problem in the mouth of the hospitalized patient. The homebound patient needs special equipment brought to the home by the hygienist and dentist. Appointment times and facilities for equipment must be arranged in advance according to the patient's individual situation.

In caring for the geriatric (elderly) patient, the hygienist must learn to recognize the changes in tissues, skin, and muscles that can affect the condition of the aging mouth. Hygienists are working more and more with older people in nursing homes and hospitals and often are the primary providers of dental care. Detailed histories of these patients are needed to know what to expect and what services to offer. Oral tissues must be carefully checked because of the frequent occurrence of oral cancer.

In this era of increased responsibilities, it is important that the hygienist continues to be recognized as a professional who is performing professional services.

CHAPTER 5

DENTAL EDUCATION

If you are considering a career as a dentist, early preparation is helpful. Concentrating on science and mathematics classes in high school will prepare you for college and also help you decide if dentistry is the best career for you. As competition is keen for the number of places in dental school, you should try for high academic standards as early as your high school years.

Courses in biology, physics, chemistry, and advanced mathematics, in addition to English and humanities courses, are the most useful. You should find out by your second or third year in high school the specific requirements of several colleges that you would like to attend to be sure you are taking the courses necessary for admission.

More than half of first-year students enter dental school with a bachelor's degree. Requirements to enter dental school vary; however, two to four years of college education is required. Specific college courses required for admission to dental school include: English, biology, general or inorganic chemistry, organic chemistry, and physics. The necessary number of credit hours in the subject area may vary, according to the requirements established by each school.

DENTAL ADMISSION TEST

All United States dental schools require that applicants take the Dental Admission Test (DAT), administered by the Division of Educational

Measurements of the Council on Dental Education, American Dental Association. The DAT is designed to assist the prospective student, his or her advisors, and the dental schools in evaluating the aptitude of the candidate.

The entire test requires one day to administer and tests the following areas:

1. knowledge of natural sciences (biology and inorganic and organic chemistry)
2. reading comprehension (natural and basic sciences)
3. verbal and quantitative ability
4. perceptual ability (two- and three-dimensional problem solving)

Dental schools apply different emphases to these parts of the test. Although there is no formal preparation for the test, students who have not taken a basic science course in more than two years are advised to review for the DAT.

The tests are given twice each year in October and April at more than a hundred locations in the United States. Advanced registration is required. Applications can be obtained from either the dental school of the student's choice or from the Division of Educational Measurements, American Dental Association.

APPLICATION FOR ADMISSION

After selecting the school or schools to which applications will be made, you should obtain application materials either from the American Association of Dental Schools (see Appendix A) or from the school itself. Although application procedures vary from school to school, in general the application process begins about one year before the date of desired admission. Although most dental schools prefer that DAT scores be available when the student applies for admission, you should not delay submission of your application simply because your DAT scores are not yet available.

Once the dental school has received the application, it will be screened and studied by an admissions committee. The committee's decision will be based on such factors as biographical and academic information supplied by the applicant, his or her undergraduate education, DAT scores, letters of recommendation, and interviews. Interview policies vary widely among the schools: some require a personal interview, some make it an option for either the applicant or the admissions committee, and some give no interviews at all.

SELECTING A SCHOOL

Selection of a dental school depends on cost, location, size, and type of program offered. Degrees offered by the dental schools in the United States are the D.M.D. (Doctor of Dental Medicine) or the more traditional D.D.S. (Doctor of Dental Surgery). Today these two degrees are equivalent and are simply different names for the same degree.

Accredited dental schools offer excellent programs; each one is reviewed regularly and accreditation ensures high standards. The Council on Dental Education of the American Dental Association has established requirements for the schools that include minimum standards for the admission of students, recommendations and guidelines for courses to be included in the curriculum, financial stability of the institution, and qualifications of the faculty members. Dental schools also are members of the American Association of Dental Schools. The association provides many services to individuals and institutions involved in dental education, including a continuing program of surveys of the needs of dental schools, faculty members, and students.

The goal of every dental school program is to produce graduates who are educated in biological and clinical sciences, capable of providing care to patients, and committed to high standards in their service. To produce these graduates, four years or more of study is required in the traditional dental schools.

See Appendix B for a list of dental schools in the United States and Canada.

DENTAL SCHOOL CURRICULUM

The majority of the first two years of dental school is spent in the study of biological sciences to learn about the function of the body and its diseases. Instruction in the basic biological sciences may be provided by the members of the medical school faculty. Oral anatomy, oral pathology, and oral histology are taught by members of the dental school faculty.

During the first two years, the student also learns the basic principles of oral diagnosis and treatment and begins study of dental treatment and procedures through practice on models of the teeth and mouth. In the final two years, students learn through clinical practice by treating patients under the supervision of clinical instructors. Students acquire clinical knowledge and experience in hospitals and other settings off and on campus.

Usually, students work in the various types of clinics of the dental school, moving from one type of dentistry to another. They learn the basic techniques involved in restorative dentistry, periodontics, oral pathology, orthodontics, pediatric dentistry, and other types of treatment that are part of a general dental practice. Students also learn to treat the chronically ill, handicapped, and older patients. In addition, most schools provide courses in practice management and effective use of assistants.

Curriculums in dental schools constantly change to stay current: new materials are introduced, new courses are given, and new techniques are developed. Some schools have adopted a four-academic/three-calendar year curriculum. Recently, in clinical training, emphasis has been put on providing more comprehensive care for patients by recognizing additional needs and meeting these needs within the practitioner's level of competence.

For nearly all of the eight specialties in dentistry, additional study is required beyond the dental degree. Graduate programs offer specialized training with more time spent treating patients. Opportunities for learning in dental schools allow students many options in shaping their dental careers.

EDUCATION FOR DENTAL HYGIENISTS

If you are interested in a career as a dental hygienist, preparation also begins in high school. As in any dental career, biology, science, and mathematics should be high on the list of priority courses; English and speech are also important, as much of a hygienist's work involves educating patients about the care of their teeth. Any course that can help develop communication skills is useful.

Nearly all dental hygiene schools receive more applications than can be accepted. You should know the specific requirements of the school you hope to enter. Some schools require a year of college for admission, while others require above average grades, and still others require experience in a dental office. Most require a satisfactory score on the Dental Hygiene Aptitude Test.

Aptitude Test

This test covers four areas of general knowledge. The first part covers numerical ability. The second part tests your knowledge of science—chemistry, physics, and biology. The third area is verbal ability and vocabulary knowledge. In the fourth part, reading comprehension is tested. The examination is given three times a year at various testing centers—usually at dental hygiene schools.

Curriculum

In school, you may choose a two-year or four-year program. The two-year program leads to a certificate in dental hygiene; some schools award an associate degree. If you wish to work in a clinic or a private office, the two-year program is adequate. The four-year program leads to a baccalaureate degree with a major in dental hygiene. If you would like a career in dental public health or in teaching, the four-year program is the better choice because of the additional courses. For advanced positions, many hygienists study for a master's degree, such as the M.S. (Master of Science) in dental hygiene education or administration, or the M.P.H. (Master of Public Health). See Appendix C for a complete list of schools offering programs in dental hygiene.

The curriculum in a two-year program includes practical clinical experience plus courses in anatomy and physiology, radiography, dental hygiene, dental materials, tooth morphology (structure) and oral anatomy, nutrition, pharmacology (medicines), pathology, and speech courses. In the four-year programs, dental hygiene, science, and liberal arts courses can be combined during the four years. Another choice is to complete the two-year program and transfer to a school that offers a postcertificate baccalaureate program. Different fields of practice require specific degrees.

EDUCATION FOR DENTAL ASSISTANTS

Until nearly thirty years ago, most dental assistants began their careers through on-the-job training, because few training programs were available. Today there are nearly three hundred approved schools that offer training courses. Courses in dental assisting are offered in many junior and community colleges or vocational and technical schools. See Appendix D for a list of these schools.

No specialized tests are given for admission to these programs, but most schools require a high school diploma or equivalency, above average grades in science and English, a high school grade point average of C or higher, and a personal interview. Some programs require applicants to take a nationally recognized college entrance examination such as the School and College Ability Test (S.C.A.T.) or the American College Test (A.C.T.), both of which are administered annually at high schools in the United States.

As in other careers in dentistry, high school courses should include science and English; in addition, speech and typing should be emphasized. These courses offer preparation and background for the courses in the training programs.

In the training schools for dental assistants, there are two types of programs: one-year programs award a certificate after successful completion and two-year programs offer a degree of Associate in Arts (A.A.) or Associate in Applied Science (A.A.S.). Courses offered in the training schools include dental anatomy, nutrition, radiography, bacteriology, laboratory procedures, clinical practice, operating room procedures, and secretarial and office routines. Trainees can obtain practical clinical experience in affiliated dental schools, local clinics, or dental offices.

EDUCATION FOR DENTAL
LABORATORY TECHNICIANS

Training for this career can be done in two ways: on the job in a commercial laboratory or in a two-year educational program. In a commercial laboratory, the program usually lasts for approximately three years, depending on the student's ability to master various laboratory techniques. During the apprenticeship period, the technician is paid. Once the training is finished, the salary is increased.

Approximately thirty accredited programs in community colleges, technical institutes, vocational schools, and dental schools provide instruction in theory and principles of dental laboratory technology. (See Appendix E for a list of programs.) Courses given the first year of instruction in these programs include work in chemistry, dental law, metallurgy, laboratory techniques, and dental ethics. During the second year, the student is given additional experience in the technology of working with small hand instruments, drills, and electrical equipment. The technician uses such materials as plastics, gold, silver, stainless steel, and porcelain in constructing dental appliances.

It is not necessary to successfully complete a formal test or examination to enter these training programs. The basic requirement is a high school diploma. However, employers or admissions personnel look for these qualifications: a high degree of manual dexterity, a well-developed sense of color perception, a concern for detail and accuracy, and patience in working with small objects.

High school courses in arts, crafts (industrial education), and basic sciences are most helpful if you are planning a career as a dental laboratory technician.

FINANCING DENTAL EDUCATION

Dental education is expensive. Costs can range from $3,000 to $20,000 or more each year. Publicly supported schools are less expensive than privately supported institutions. Tuition at the schools is not the only expense; instruments, books, and uniforms must also be included.

Students who apply for admission to dental schools must be prepared for these relatively high costs. In addition, because the academic schedule is rigorous and demanding, most schools advise against holding down a job during the school year. All schools have funds to provide financial assistance and will furnish information on the availability of that aid. Students should also investigate sources in their community. Service organizations, public and private loans, dental associations, state or federally guaranteed loans, and various types of scholarships can be useful sources of information and financial assistance. The following are some sources of financial aid.

Federal Guaranteed Student Loan Program

This program makes it possible for students to borrow from private lenders to help pay the cost of schools; the federal government pays part of the interest. Loans are guaranteed either by state or private nonprofit agencies or insured by the federal government. Students may borrow up to $5,500 annually up to a total of $65,500 for graduate study. Repayment begins usually nine to twelve months after the student leaves school, but payment may be deferred for military or other service or additional study.

National Health Service Corps Scholarship Program

These scholarships are available for dental students of exceptional financial need. For each year of academic training during which students receive the scholarship, they must provide one year of public service; a minimum of two years is required. Individuals are assigned to the National Health Service Corps, Indian Health Service, Public Health Service hospitals and clinics, Coast Guard medical facilities, federal prison medical facilities, or private practice in an understaffed area.

Health Professions Student Loan Program

These loans have a low interest rate and can be made for as much as the cost of tuition plus $2,500 or more each year. Applications can be made directly from the dental school. Loans are repayable during a ten-year period that begins one year after a student stops full-time study at a dental school. Deferments of three years are possible if a student joins the armed forces or the Peace Corps or begins advanced professional training. Part of these loans may be repaid by the federal government if the graduate practices in an underserved area.

Health Education Assistance Loan Program

In this program, students may borrow as much as $20,000 per year, up to a total of $80,000 from an eligible lender (financial or credit institution, dental school, a state agency, or pension fund). These loans are insured by the federal government. The money is repayable during a ten- to fifteen-year period, starting nine months after training is completed. Again, repayment of the loan may be deferred during periods of up to three years of internship or residency training or service in the armed forces, National Health Service Corps, Peace Corps, or VISTA. Interest may be deferred while the student is in training.

The Stafford Loan

The Stafford Loan is made by a lender such as a bank, credit union, or savings and loan association. The loans are insured by the guaranteeing agency in the borrower's state. Graduate students may borrow up to $8,000 a year for the entire period of graduate study but may not exceed an aggregate maximum of $23,000 undergraduate, $65,000 graduate. New borrowers pay up to 8.25 percent interest. A 3 percent origination fee is deducted from each loan payment and passed on to the federal government to help reduce the cost to the government of subsidizing the loans.

Repayment begins six months after the borrower leaves school or falls below half-time enrollment. The borrower must contact the lender to set up a repayment schedule. The borrower may have five to ten years to repay the loan, depending on the repayment schedule. Repayment can be deferred under certain circumstances, as when the borrower serves in the armed forces, Commissioned Corps of the U.S. Public Health Service, Peace Corps, or VISTA, or for periods of unemployment, disability, or return to full-time study.

PLUS and SLS Loans

PLUS and SLS loans are part of the guaranteed student loan program. PLUS loans are made by banks, credit unions, and savings and loan associations to parents; Supplemental Loans for Students are made to students.

PLUS enables parents to borrow up to the cost of attendance, less other aid received, for each dependent child enrolled at least half time.

There is a 3 percent origination fee for these loans, and the state guarantee agency may charge an insurance premium of up to 3 percent of the loan principal, to be deducted proportionately from each loan payment. SLS and PLUS loans disbursed after July 1, 1999, have a variable interest rate, adjusted each year. The interest rate for the 1998–1999 year was 9 percent. Repayment may be deferred for SLS borrowers just as it is for Staffords; PLUS borrowers qualify for the same deferments under certain conditions.

For more information on federal programs, order the free publication, *The Student Guide: Five Federal Financial Aid Programs,* by writing to: Federal Student Aid Programs, Department DEA-86, Pueblo, CO 81009.

Scholarship for Health Professions Students of Exceptional Financial Need

A program of federal scholarships is available for dental students of "exceptional financial need." The scholarships are limited to first-year students and cover costs of tuition and other educational expenses. In addition, recipients receive a small, monthly stipend. These scholarships are available through individual dental schools.

Southern Regional Education Board

Students who are residents of participating southern states may apply for aid from the Southern Regional Education Board Regional Contract Program. Each participating state pays the dental schools a supplementary fee to help meet the cost of dental education, and thus reduce the tuition cost to the individual.

Western Interstate Commission for Higher Education

Students who are residents of western states without dental schools may apply to this Student Exchange Program. All western dental schools except Colorado participate as cooperating schools in the exchange programs. The home state pays a support fee to the dental school to help meet the cost of dental education. The student pays resident tuition in a public dental school and reduced tuition in a private school.

Other Loan Programs

Although some of the loan programs listed here are applicable only to students in dental schools, federally guaranteed loan programs are available to almost all students enrolled in accredited training programs. Many awards and scholarships are geared to help women and minority students. The costs of the programs available for hygienists, assistants, and laboratory technicians vary considerably. Costs of education for dental hygienists can be nearly as much as dental school, if the student decides on graduate work. Obviously, the cost of the dental assistants' program is lower, as less time is required for training. Also, tuition at a community college can be as little as $30 to $50 for a course, or as much as $5,000 for a fall semester at a college or university. As all but seven or eight of the fifty approved training programs for laboratory technicians are at community or junior colleges, technical schools, or institutes, the cost is much lower than that of attending a four-year program.

If you choose to follow a career in one of the dental fields, some type of financial aid can probably be found. As a final method, loans from a commercial lending institution can be an investment in your future. However, all other types of aid should first be investigated with the help of a vocational counselor at a high school or college.

The financial aid picture is constantly changing, and it is absolutely essential to meet with financial aid counselors and vocational counselors regularly to keep up with changes in scholarship, grant, loan, and award-funding programs.

The funding that was available last year may not be available this year, and new methods may have to be found.

CHAPTER 6

PROFESSIONAL COMMITMENT

A dental career is a highly professional one. A person entering such a career is engaged in one of the learned professions. *Webster's Ninth New Collegiate Dictionary* defines *professional* as "characterized by or conforming to the technical or ethical standards of a profession." The commitment to a dental career, whether as a dentist, hygienist, assistant, or laboratory technician, involves adopting all of these established professional standards.

These standards have been set by members of four organizations: the American Dental Association, the American Dental Hygienists' Association, the American Dental Assistants Association, and the National Association of Dental Laboratories. Each association has worked to establish such standards as licensing and certification, accreditation, codes of ethics, and continuing education. A look at some of these standards will help define the professionalism of dentistry.

LICENSURE

Dental Licensure

Before a dentist can legally treat patients, his or her qualifications must be approved by a government agency. The process by which a government agency approves the dentist's qualifications is called dental licensure; the credential awarded is a dental license. Dental licenses are awarded by individual states, districts, and dependencies. A license awarded by one area permits the recipient to practice only in that location. For example, dentists licensed in Illinois cannot practice in New York until they obtain a license from New York.

Licensure requirements vary from state to state, but all are similar in some respects. They consist of an educational requirement, a written examination requirement, and a clinical examination requirement. The government agency that issues dental licenses is usually the state board of dental examiners.

Most states recognize, for written examinations, the results of the National Board dental examinations. The National Board program is operated by the Commission on National Dental Examinations of the American Dental Association. There are eleven National Board examinations, Part I includes four tests of knowledge about basic sciences and dental anatomy, while Part II includes seven tests on dental specialties and pharmacology. Each test consists of approximately a hundred multiple choice items. These tests are scheduled three times a year.

In addition to these written examinations, all candidates for licensure must pass a clinical examination in which specific procedures must be performed. Usually, the candidate must supply the necessary instruments and bring a patient needing the prescribed treatment. A licensing jurisdiction may also require candidates to be of sound moral character; this documentation may vary from state to state. Many jurisdictions require proficiency in conversational English.

Dental Hygienists' Licensure

Dental hygienists must also obtain a license before practicing. After graduation from an accredited program, the hygienist candidate must take the written National Board Examination, which consists of tests on basic sciences; dental anatomy, histology, and pathology; pharmacology; nutrition; dental materials; radiology; and preventive dentistry. The candidate must also pass a state or regional clinical (practical) examination.

The candidate must pass both the written and clinical examinations and be licensed by the State Board of Dental Examiners in the state selected for practice. Most states accept the National Board Examination for the written tests; those that do not provide their own written examinations. Until recently, a dental hygienist had to take a clinical examination for each state in which she or he wanted to practice. However, regional examining boards, which include a group or an area of states, have established tests accepted by the groups. Most states do require a written test on the State Dental Practice Act. After all tests are successfully completed, the hygienist is classified as R.D.H. (Registered Dental Hygienist).

The rapid growth in the scope of dental hygiene has led some states to require that candidates be tested in new procedures for which they may be responsible. These may include placing, polishing, and removing temporary and other restorations; performing gingival curettage (surgical cleaning); administering anesthesia; and other functions. In many states, an additional requirement for continued licensure is that a certain number of continuing education credits be earned each year.

Dental Assistants' Certification

The dental assistant is not licensed but certified. Requirements for certification include graduation from an accredited dental assisting program and successful completion of the certification examination of the Certifying Board of the American Dental Assistants Association. The examination is not a requirement for practice, but is taken voluntarily to verify the assistant's competence. The written test covers theory and knowledge of laboratory methods and techniques, basic and dental science, radiology, and functions of the assistant. Standard clinical procedures are also part of the examination.

After the examination is successfully completed, the assistant holds the title of Certified Dental Assistant (C.D.A.). By participation in a continuing education program, the assistant can continue to achieve certification status annually. As the duties of assistants continue to expand, licensure or registration of all dental assistants in every state may become a reality.

Dental Laboratory Technicians' Certification

The certification program for technicians was founded in 1958 by the National Association of Dental Laboratories in cooperation with the

Council on Dental Education, American Dental Association. The program, according to the National Association of Dental Laboratories, is designed to bring recognition to the highly qualified, ethical dental technician, provide continuing advanced educational opportunities, and raise the overall technical and ethical performance standards of the dental laboratory industry and craft.

Candidates for the Certified Dental Technician (C.D.T.) must take a written examination that covers history, ethics, and jurisprudence in the dental laboratory industry, plus techniques, procedures, and materials needed in laboratory specialties. Tests consist of multiple choice questions. Preliminary laboratory work is required; instructions and materials are provided to candidates four weeks before the testing session. This work is brought to the examination by the candidate.

C.D.T. candidates must have a high school education or equivalent. Five years of experience is required. Time spent in approved supervised training in a dental laboratory school may be substituted for part of the experience. Certified dental technicians must renew their certification every year by meeting continuing education requirements and must attest to their continuing ethical standards.

ACCREDITATION

Dental schools and programs listed as *accredited* have met standards and criteria established by a national organization. Standards on curriculum, faculty, and other factors are established; schools and training programs are visited regularly by qualified representatives to ensure the standards are met.

The Commission on Dental Accreditation of the American Dental Association is responsible for granting accreditation status. For all of the institutions listed in the appendixes of this book, some classification of accreditation was granted as of June 1989. These classifications can vary, according to the length of time the program has been in operation or how well the program has succeeded in graduating qualified persons.

The list of schools and programs cannot be complete, as there are always additional programs under development or in the early stages of operation. The purpose of the entire accreditation system is to ensure high educational standards for students in the schools and training programs.

ADA CODE OF ETHICS

Another means to ensure high standards for the dental profession is to establish codes of conduct for its members. The "Code of Ethics and Code of Professional Conduct" of the American Dental Association lists three characteristics of a profession in the preamble to the code: "the primary duty of service to the public, education beyond the usual level, and the responsibility for self-government."

Some highlights of the code of the American Dental Association are:

Principle-section 1

Service to the public and quality of care. The dentist's primary professional obligation shall be service to the public. The competent and timely delivery of quality care within the bounds of the clinical circumstances presented by the patient, with due consideration being given to the needs and desires of the patient, shall be the most important aspect of that obligation.

CODE OF PROFESSIONAL CONDUCT

Patient selection. While dentists, in serving the public, may exercise reasonable discretion in selecting patients for their practices, dentists shall not refuse to accept patients into their practice or deny dental service to patients because of the patient's race, creed, color, sex, or national origin.

Patient records. Dentists are obliged to safeguard the confidentiality of patient records. Dentists shall maintain patient records in a manner consistent with the protection of the welfare of the patient. Upon request of a patient or another dental practitioner, dentists shall provide any information that will be beneficial for the future treatment of the patient.

Community service. Since dentists have an obligation to use their skills, knowledge, and experience for the improvement of the dental health of the public and are encouraged to be leaders in their community, dentists in such service shall conduct themselves in such a manner as to maintain or elevate the esteem of the profession.

Emergency service. Dentists shall be obliged to make reasonable arrangements for the emergency care of their patients of record.

Dentists shall be obliged when consulted in an emergency by patients not of record to make reasonable arrangements for emergency care. If treatment is provided, the dentist, upon completion of such treatment, is obliged to return the patient to his or her regular dentist unless the patient expressly reveals a different preference.

Consultation and referral. Dentists shall be obliged to seek consultation, if possible, whenever the welfare of patients will be safeguarded or advanced by utilizing those who have special skills, knowledge, and experience. When patients visit or are referred to specialists or consulting dentists for consultation:

- The specialists or consulting dentists upon completion of their care shall return the patient, unless the patient expressly reveals a different preference, to the referring dentist, or if none, to the dentist of record for future care.
- The specialists shall be obliged when there is no referring dentist and upon a completion of their treatment to inform patients when there is a need for further dental care.

Use of auxiliary personnel. Dentists shall be obliged to protect the health of their patients by only assigning to qualified auxiliaries those duties which can be legally delegated. Dentists shall be further obliged to prescribe and supervise the work of all auxiliary personnel working under their direction and control.

Justifiable criticism and expert testimony. Dentists shall be obliged to report to the appropriate reviewing agency instances of gross or continual faulty treatment by other dentists. Patients should be informed of their present oral health status without disparaging comment about prior services. Dentists issuing a public statement with respect to the profession shall have a reasonable basis to believe that the comments made are true. Dentists may provide expert testimony when that testimony is essential to a just and fair disposition of a judicial or administration action.

Rebate and split fees. Dentists shall not accept or tender "rebates" or "split fees."

Representation of care and fees. Dentists shall not represent the care being rendered to their patients or the fees being charged for providing such care in a false or misleading manner.

Principle-section 2

Education. The privilege of dentists to be accorded professional status rests primarily in the knowledge, skill, and experience with which they serve their patients and society. All dentists, therefore, have the obligation of keeping their knowledge and skill current.

Principle-section 3

Government of a profession. Every profession owes society the responsibility to regulate itself. Such regulation is achieved largely through the influence of the professional societies. All dentists, therefore, have the dual obligation of making themselves a part of a professional society and of observing its rules of ethics.

Principle-section 4

Research and development. Dentists have the obligation of making the results and benefits of their investigative efforts available to all when they are useful in safeguarding or promoting the health of the public.

Devices and therapeutic methods. Except for formal investigative studies, dentists shall be obliged to prescribe, dispense, or promote only those devices, drugs and other agents whose complete formulae are available to the dental profession. Dentists shall have the further obligation of not holding out as exclusive any device, agent, method, or technique.

Patents and copyrights. Patents and copyrights may be secured by dentists provided that such patents and copyrights shall not be used to restrict research or practice.

Principle-section 5

Professional announcement. In order to properly serve the public, dentists should represent themselves in a manner that contributes to the esteem of the profession. Dentists should not misrepresent their training and competence in any way that would be false or misleading in any material respect.

Advertising. Although any dentist may advertise, no dentist shall advertise or solicit patients in any form of communication in a manner that is false or misleading in any material respect.

Name of practice. Since the name under which a dentist conducts her or his practice may be a factor in the selection process of the patient, the use of a trade name or an assumed name that is false or misleading in any material respect is unethical.

Use of the name of a dentist no longer actively associated with the practice may be continued for a period not to exceed one year.

Announcement of specialization and limitation of practice. The special areas of dental practice approved by the American Dental Association and the designation for ethical specialty announcement and limitation of practice are: dental public health, endodontics, oral pathology, oral and maxillofacial surgery, orthodontics, pediatric dentistry, periodontics, and prosthodontics.

Dentists who choose to announce specialization should use "specialist in" or "practice limited to" and shall limit their practice exclusively to the announced special area(s) of dental practice, provided at the time of the announcement such dentists have met in each approved specialty for which they announce the existing educational requirements and standards set forth by the American Dental Association.

Dentists who use their eligibility to announce as specialists to make the public believe that specialty services rendered in the dental office are being rendered by qualified specialists when such is not the case are engaged in unethical conduct. The burden of responsibility is on specialists to avoid any inference that general practitioners who are associated with specialists are qualified to announce themselves as specialists.

General standards

The special area(s) of dental practice and an appropriate certifying board must be approved by the American Dental Association.

Dentists who announce themselves as specialists must have successfully completed an educational program accredited by the Commission on Dental Accreditation or be diplomates of an American Dental Association recognized certifying board. The scope of the individual specialist's practice shall be governed by the educational standards for the speciality in which the specialist is announcing.

The practice carried on by dentists who announce as specialists shall be limited exclusively to the special area(s) of dental practices announced by the dentist.

Standards for multiple specialty announcements. Educational criteria for announcement by dentists in additional recognized specialty areas are the successful completion of an educational program accredited by the Commission on Dental Accreditation in each area for which the dentist wishes to announce.

Dentists who completed their advanced education in programs listed by the Council on Dental Education prior to the initiation of the accreditation process in 1967 and who are currently ethically announcing as specialists in a recognized area may announce in additional areas provided they are educationally qualified or are certified diplomates in each area for which they wish to announce. Documentation of successful completion of the educational program(s) must be submitted to the appropriate constituent society. The documentation must assure that the duration of the program(s) is a minimum of two years except for oral and maxillofacial surgery which must have been a minimum of three years in duration.

General practitioner announcement of services. General dentists who wish to announce the services available in their practices are permitted to announce the availability of those services so long as they avoid any communications that express or imply specialization. General dentists shall also state that the services are being provided by general dentists. No dentist shall announce available services in any way that would be false or misleading in any material respect.

ADHA PRINCIPLES

Each member of the American Dental Hygienists' Association has the ethical obligation to subscribe to the following principles:

- To provide oral health care utilizing highest professional knowledge, judgment, and ability.
- To serve all patients without discrimination.

- To hold professional patient relationships in confidence.
- To utilize every opportunity to increase public understanding of oral health practices.
- To generate public confidence in members of the dental health professions.
- To cooperate with all health professions in meeting the health needs of the public.
- To recognize and uphold the laws and regulations governing this profession.
- To participate responsibly in this professional Association and uphold its purpose.
- To maintain professional competence through continuing education.
- To exchange professional knowledge with other health professions.
- To represent dental hygiene with high standards of personal conduct.

ADAA PRINCIPLES

Every member of the American Dental Assistants Association shall have the obligation to:

- Hold in confidence the details of professional services rendered by an employer and the confidences of any patient.
- Increase abilities and skills by seeking additional education in the dental assisting field, through services provided by this Association, the constituent associations, and component societies.
- Participate actively in the efforts of this Association and the constituent associations and component societies to improve the educational status of the dental assistant.
- Refrain from performing any service for patients which requires the professional competence of a dentist, or is prohibited by the dental practice act of the state in which the member is employed.
- Support these Principles of Ethics and the Pledge.

The following is the official pledge of the association. It was written by Dr. Charles Nelson of Chicago, who was the first advisor to the Association. "I solemnly pledge that, in the practice of my profession, I will always be loyal to the welfare of the patients who come under my care, and to the interest of the practitioner whom I serve. I will be just and generous to the members of my profession, aiding them and lending them encouragement to be loyal, to be just, to be studious. I hereby pledge to devote my best energies to the service of humanity in that relationship of life to which I consecrated myself when I elected to become a dental assistant."

NADL CODE

The preamble to the National Association of Dental Laboratories (NADL) code states that "the future of all those engaged in the dental laboratory industry depends to a great extent upon the maintenance of high standards of business conduct and a harmonious relationship with members of the dental profession.... These canons of ethics are adopted as a general guide...."

Advertising

Section 1. Advertising by members of this Association shall at all times be directed solely to duly qualified members of the dental profession. Advertising in magazines, journals, and bulletins should be confined to media which is distributed only to members of the profession, dental laboratories, dental manufacturers, and others directly connected with the industry.

Section 2. Prices should not be advertised except to members of the profession or to commercial dental laboratories and then only in sealed communications.

Section 3. Advertising must be honest and in no way untrue, deceptive, or misleading.

Section 4. Signs may be used at the place of business of any member provided that they are not of such size or nature as to attract attention of the general public.

Materials

Section 1. Members shall use only such materials as are specified by the dentist for whom the work is being performed. If the choice of materials is left to the discretion of the member, upon written request, he will accurately inform the dentist respecting the type and kind of material used.

Section 2. Upon request each member shall furnish with every new completed dental appliance a fully itemized invoice showing the name of the material used.

General Conduct

Section 1. Members shall not render or aid others in rendering any service directly to the general public. This shall not prejudice the right of any member to construct specimens or other appliances for dentists, dental dealers, or manufacturers when the same are to be used solely for technical or display purposes.

Section 2. No member shall defame, malign, or falsely accuse any other dental laboratory or any dentist of dishonorable conduct, inability to perform services, or make any other false representation which will tend to degrade such person.

Section 3. Members of this Association shall not conspire with others to fix prices in violation of antitrust laws or any law governing fair trade practices.

CONTINUING EDUCATION

An important part of the professionalism of any career is the desire to keep gaining knowledge. For all phases of dentistry, new techniques, methods, and materials are being developed, and the professional person keeps up to date. One of the most effective ways to keep current is through continuing education.

Courses in continuing education are offered, in most instances, by the four associations involved. They are given in the form of classes at a university or community college, in study groups, and at scientific sessions of the associations involved. Courses can be one-day, all-day sessions or seminars that continue for several weeks and range in subject matter from practice management to infection control techniques.

Anyone truly interested in maintaining a professional attitude will want to take part in an educational experience that will increase skills and ability and will ultimately, of course, benefit patients' dental health.

CHAPTER 7

GETTING STARTED

As you consider the satisfactions and rewards of a dental career, you should take time to evaluate your personal qualifications. Try to judge honestly which of the following qualities you have to meet the goal of a dental career. An evaluation of your personal merits and motivations can help you make your career selection.

PERSONAL MOTIVATIONS

Commitment to a goal. You should be able to reach a decision on which part of dentistry appeals to you and be able to use the steps outlined in this book to achieve that goal.

Willingness to train. You must be able to choose your school, your program, and your schedule for training for your determined goal. You must be willing to make sacrifices in your time and money.

Interest in science. You must have this interest, as all phases of dentistry require knowledge, enthusiasm, and curiosity about science—ranging from basic sciences to the details of research.

Ability to work hard. In many instances, you may have to work irregular hours with time extending longer than a forty-hour week. Certainly, in your school or training program, long hours of work plus study will be necessary.

Concern for people. In dentistry, patients will need your reassurance and concern about the state of their oral health. If you do not believe that you can have this concern, you may not want to consider seriously a career in a health-oriented profession in which you work with patients.

Achievement in scholarship. You must be able to achieve grades that are above average in order to be accepted in an accredited program. If you establish the pattern of good study habits, you will be able to attain the necessary grades more easily.

Dexterity in manual skills. Part of the Dental Admissions Test identifies factors in perceptual ability that predict manual ability. The test has been effective in selecting candidates who can perform delicate manual tasks. As so many dental procedures depend on manual dexterity, you can check your ability by working with hand tools to create a small model in wood, plaster, clay, or any similar material.

Ability to communicate. You need communication skills to describe a proposed treatment to a patient, to educate the patient in the best oral hygiene practices, or to reassure a nervous patient. You can communicate with your voice, your body language, and your facial expressions. You must be aware of how best to deal with each patient's needs and how to respond to these needs.

Continued desire to learn. In each phase of dentistry discussed in this book, continuing education has been emphasized. If you think this type of effort is wasted, you need to reconsider. New developments and technologies must be learned for the greater benefit of the profession and the patients it serves.

Cooperation with others. Dentistry is not a profession for hermits. In no part of it can you work alone. Even if you choose a career such as a dental laboratory technician, you will interact with your supervisors and other coworkers. Getting along with people on all levels is an important asset to any career. Becoming part of a group in which you can interact with your peers or with people older or younger than you will sharpen this skill.

PSYCHOLOGY OF DENTISTRY

In analyzing your motivations for entering dentistry, you have been engaged in a psychological self-examination. Psychology needs a separate section of its own in this chapter because of its importance in dental care. Psychology can be defined as a study of the mind and behavior and this knowledge is essential to those who want to practice in dentistry.

Dentistry by its nature is extremely personal; physical closeness is involved in the treatment. Dealing with people at close range means that you must be aware of the sensitivities of patients and provide treatment with cheerfulness and concern for the patient's well-being.

Many patients arrive at the dental office in a state of apprehension. They may be nervous because of a previous painful experience, because they have neglected their dental care, or because they are in pain and need treatment. The dental team must understand how to deal with any and all of these problems.

Negative feelings about teeth can be traced to the discomfort involved when a child's teeth are erupting—a sometimes painful process. Loss of primary teeth or accidental injury again focuses on pain. If the appearance of the first cavity in the mouth is associated with a trip to the dentist where the child is told that all the sugar-containing foods he or she enjoys are bad for the teeth, it follows that the dentist is someone to be avoided. These negative feelings can carry over to adult life and habits.

Superstitions contribute to these negative feelings. Folk wisdom about the loss of a tooth by the expectant mother for each child born is still prevalent in many parts of our society. People also believe that they must lose their teeth as they grow older. This has come to be accepted as part of the aging process. Developing positive attitudes against these negative feelings is difficult.

Not enough people think of the dentist as a person who provides preventive care. The dentist is associated with removal of teeth, drilling, anesthetics, and repair, rather than with comfort and ease of pain. The treatment is also regarded as expensive, and many people use this as an excuse for not visiting the dentist regularly.

Thanks to the dental profession's emphasis on preventive care and good oral hygiene, plus the fluoridation of water, today's teenagers have fewer cavities than did the same group twenty years ago. The new technological advances—high-speed dental drills, anesthetics, and antibiotics—make dental care quite painless.

To overcome the patient's negative images and feelings, the dentist and staff members must have some techniques to effect a change in attitude. The techniques can be studied and applied by any professional in dealing with patients.

Technical Skills

These skills are acquired in the training programs for dental professionals and must be applied with confidence. The skills must not be displayed with an attitude of superiority, but with a desire to help the patient by using these skills. If the patient believes that the professional is well qualified, he or she can relax more easily.

Effective Communication

This is the most important technique to acquire. The dentist and staff members must be aware of the whole person and communicate accordingly. Each patient represents a different set of emotions and motivations. Some patients can be given a logical explanation for their proposed treatment; others need an emotional response.

Patients who are money-conscious need to have treatment explained in terms of amounts saved over a time period. The aesthetic appearance of their teeth should be emphasized to those concerned primarily with appearance. Studying the patient for the best approach involves listening to the patient express his or her needs as the first part of the communication process.

The second part of the communication exchange is responding to the patient's expressed needs. Staff members must find a point of agreement and use that as the basis for reply. The point can be expanded to draw the patient into more discussion until a decision favorable to both persons has been reached. If the staff member is determined to assert a personal opinion, regardless of the effect on the patient, communication is lost in a one-way street. The patient becomes closed to further discussion and probably is lost to the practice.

Some patients may never be reconciled to settling differences and may be dismissed from the dentist's practice. More often, a misunderstanding can be cleared up by an open, two-way discussion.

Involvement of Patient

To motivate a patient to use preventive dentistry practices, the dental staff must find the right approach. A logical approach does not always work. People may be aware of the causes of dental decay but may not follow preventive procedures any more than they consistently fasten seat belts in automobiles.

The right approach, then, is the one that appeals to the patient. Often, participation will work. If the patient can use a brush with use of a model or floss while the hygienist is explaining the technique, the lesson will be reinforced.

Visual reinforcement with pictures and drawings will also help. Emphasize the effects of oral disease. Offer immediate and long-term goals for the patient to achieve. Put the patient in first place; it is the patient, not the dentist, who is the prime provider of dental health. Emphasize the outcome—an attractive smile.

In a study reported in *The Journal of the American Dental Association**, patients said that the chief reasons for anxiety about visiting the dentist's office were lack of communication between the dentist and patient, perceived lack of control in the dentist's operatory, and fear of being criticized for not taking care of their teeth.

Many new methods of treating fearful patients are currently in use. Behavioral techniques include patient relaxation, systemic desensitization, hypnosis, and meeting with the patient in a nonclinical setting to discuss the patient's concerns. A number of universities, medical centers, and hospitals have clinics to treat dentally anxious patients. If psychology is not a requirement in your training program, put it at the top of your list of electives.

---

*McCann, D. "Dental phobia: conquering fear with trust." *Journal of the American Dental Association* (1989): 593–598.

CHECKLIST

As you plan for a career in dentistry, here is a checklist of suggested steps to follow. Not all are applicable to each situation, but they provide a means to organize your intended lifestyle.

1. In high school, take as many science courses as possible. In addition, take typing courses to provide yourself with a useful tool.
2. Visit a dental office to observe and ask questions. Ask if you can shadow someone for a day.
3. Select a training program or college early enough to plan to meet entrance requirements.
4. Write to SELECT at the American Dental Association for detailed information on dental careers.
5. If you choose to enter dental school, follow all necessary steps for a better chance of acceptance.
6. Investigate all types of financial aid available for training programs.
7. In school, determine the specialization or practice that interests you most.
8. Decide on the geographic location and type of community you prefer.
9. Subscribe to professional journals and check their advertising pages.
10. Register with the placement counselor at your school.
11. Arrange for references.
12. After you have completed your degree or finished your training, prepare to find a job. Check out *Resumes for College Students and Recent Graduates* by VGM Career Books for helpful examples of winning resumes.
13. Use these suggestions to help with the job hunt.
14. Get ready for the job interview. *How to Have a Winning Job Interview* by VGM Career Books offers expert advice on all aspects of the interview process.

1. Take the Right Courses

If you are going to enter a dental career, it is important to find out soon if science appeals to you. Courses in biology, physics, and chemistry will confirm or disprove your interest. Typing will help you in your classroom programs when reports are required and in an office situation when typing can be part of office skills.

2. Visit a Dental Office

Take a closer look at the office you've been visiting as a patient. Look at the equipment used and the various duties performed by the dentist, hygienist, assistant, and laboratory technician. Watch the teamwork of the personnel. Ask them questions about their jobs, their training, and why they chose their professions.

3. Select an Educational Program

Many training programs and colleges have specific entrance requirements. General requirements for admission to most colleges and universities include graduation from high school in the upper third or fourth of the graduating class and a total of 15 or 16 units in these subjects:

English, 3 to 4 units
mathematics, 3 to 4 units
science, 2 to 3 units
social studies, 1 to 2 units
foreign language, 1 to 2 units
others, 1 to 2 units (history, typing, psychology, other electives)

In addition, scores from scholastic aptitude tests and other specialized tests will be considered in your application, along with recommendations from teachers, your extracurricular activities, and personal qualifications.

Your high school counselors have available bulletins from many institutions for higher education that will give you specific information. Your choice may be determined by many factors: location, cost, size. You may prefer a small private school as opposed to a large state-supported program. In any case, visit the campus and talk to students in the school. Visit several schools before you make your choice. Most colleges hold special visitation days when you can stay on campus and attend classes and social events.

4. Select

In the 1980s, the American Dental Association and the American Association of Dental Schools started a program called SELECT to attract capable individuals to careers in the dental profession. Every state dental society and dental school has a SELECT representative who can provide accurate information about dental careers. The national SELECT office provides detailed information in the form of brochures, fact sheets, posters, videotapes, and lists of accredited schools. The address is: SELECT, American Dental Association, Suite 1804, 211 East Chicago Avenue, Chicago, Illinois 60611.

5. Choose a Dental School

The American Association of Dental Schools has a uniform application in a standardized format used by many dental schools. The association acts as a clearinghouse for these applications. If you plan to apply to dental school, you may obtain this form and use it to apply to those schools where you think your application will be the most successful. The association publishes *Admission Requirements of U.S. and Canadian Dental Schools*, which provides extensive information on the schools' curriculums, expenses, and other data.

The fee for using the association's application service is $85 for the first school and $10 for each additional school. You will be required to write an essay as part of the application service and to mail letters of recommendation directly to each school.

Decisions for acceptance of your application will be based on information from you and the undergraduate school, Dental Admission Test scores, recommendation letters, and interviews. Policies about the personal interview may vary; some schools require one, others offer it as an option, and some hold no personal interviews.

6. Investigate Financial Aid

Although the costs of dental training are high, you should consider the cost a good investment for your future. Meet with your school's vocational counselor, and determine with your family and the counselor what resources are available to you. Many scholarship funds are overlooked because not enough people are aware of them. For example, there may be sources of aid in your own community through citizen groups or service organizations. There are special scholarships available for dental students if they provide public service after graduation. Applications for loans and scholarships can be obtained from the financial aid offices of each school.

If you look at the investment of money as a source of increased income for you, the cost seems worthwhile, but the expense of dental training may represent a sacrifice for both you and your family.

7. Determine Your Specialization

In dental school, you have a choice of training for general dentistry or for one of the eight specialties of dentistry described in Chapter 3. If you are in a program for hygienists, you may decide on training for general practice or one of the eight specialties. You may investigate a teaching career, hospital service, work abroad, or other types of practice.

There are also options for the dental assistant. You may decide that one of the specialties is more appealing than another and take extra courses in that field, you may take additional office training to become an office manager, or you may decide to complete degree requirements to become a teacher.

If you have entered a laboratory technician training program, you can decide if you want to work independently in a dental office, as part of a commercial laboratory, or for various governmental agencies such as the military services.

8. Choose a Location

When you have a skill to offer, your ability to choose your geographic location is much greater than if you have to take any available job. If you are considering a position in a community new to you, visit it for a look at what it offers in recreation, housing, educational opportunities, or whatever fits your lifestyle. As this will be your environment for at least several years, do not make this decision hastily.

9. Subscribe to Professional Journals

These journals can be a source of information about the types and location of job opportunities. Some of the journals contain classified advertising. Each phase of dentistry has at least one journal devoted to the interest groups; for example, *Dental Hygiene, The Dental Assistant, Dental Teamwork, Trends and Techniques in the Contemporary Dental Laboratory,* and *The Journal of the American Dental Association.*

10. Register with a Placement Officer

Nearly every college and training program has a full-time staff person who can help you find a position. Some placement offices act as a service to send transcripts and other records for you. Other placement offices post announcements of positions available and keep informed about vacancies that occur, both in nearby communities and in other states.

11. Get References

Never offer a name for reference to a prospective employer unless you have first asked permission to use that person's name. References are important, and most employers use them as a factor in making a decision. Use the names of those for whom you may have worked in a summer job. Perhaps a teacher or professor who has praised your work will be able to give you a reference. Be sure the person you ask is a responsible person who knows you well and will respond quickly to a request for a reference.

If you are using a placement service, your references can be sent there and copied as needed to send to prospective employers. In this way, only one copy of each letter of reference is needed.

12. Prepare for Job Hunting

Organize the materials necessary for job hunting. Have copies of transcripts, special awards, letters of application, and your resume. You should have several positions lined up and apply for them. Keep copies of your letters, and be ready to follow up on a reply or interview.

Your resume is one of the most important items you may ever prepare. It gives employers their first look at you, and its neatness and thoroughness make the initial impression. You may change your letter of application and resume according to the type of position. But they must be typed with no errors and reproduced in a manner easy to read.

The resume should contain your personal history in a chronological order. It should present your education, work experience, goals, personal data, special interests, awards and accomplishments, and one or two references. This should be on one typed sheet that must have your name, address, and phone number listed at the top of the page. If necessary, have the resume done by a computer service that can use different sizes of type to fit the information into a one-page format.

Your letters of application must also be neatly typed. In each one, include information about yourself that makes you qualified for the position; be self-confident without being self-centered. Ask for an interview. If you receive no reply after two weeks, write again. Enclose a copy of your resume each time.

13. The Job Hunt Itself

Occasionally the perfect job will fall right into your lap, but usually dental care professionals must take an active role in seeking a new position. Here are some avenues to pursue in your job hunt.

NEWSPAPERS

Many dentists prefer not to use newspaper ads, and those who do often use a "blind ad" when looking for new employees, which requires that you respond to a post office box. This allows the dentist to remain anonymous and puts the job applicant at a distinct disadvantage. You might find yourself applying for positions you don't want. If you are already employed, you may be sending a resume to someone whom you would rather didn't know your intentions. However, it is still a good idea to check newspapers on a daily basis. Classified ads from many of the nation's prominent newspapers are listed online with Careerpath.com.

ONLINE SOURCES

Since online employment resources are expanding rapidly, you can start your job hunt by conducting a keyword search for employment resources on popular Internet search sites such as Yahoo!, Infoseek, Lycos, AltaVista, or Webcrawler. Some of these Internet search engines maintain their own extensive employment listings. Visit the websites of the appropriate professional associations for your field. They maintain job banks and list other helpful resources.

UNSOLICITED COVER LETTERS, RESUMES, PHONE CALLS, AND NETWORKING

A quick look through the phone book will give you an idea of the number of dental offices in your area. If there aren't too many, make a quick phone call to inquire about openings. Or you might consider sending a cover letter and resume to each practice. You might get lucky and have one land in an office with a new, unadvertised opening. Be sure to include in your cover letter a statement of flexibility, such as a willingness to work nontraditional hours or to substitute—it will make you more marketable—and ask that your resume be kept on file in case of future openings. During the phone call, provide the same information and ask if you can send in a resume.

If a dentist you contact is not looking for a dental hygienist, ask him or her to pass your resume on to a colleague who may be hiring. Dental supply representatives also are excellent resources. They visit offices on a routine basis and usually are knowledgeable about current employment situations. Dental supply reps are concerned with creating and maintaining good will, and most are happy to help.

DENTAL AUXILIARY PLACEMENT SERVICE

Most metropolitan areas have dental auxiliary placement services. Fee arrangements vary among agencies. Some charge the employer, some the employee, and some divide the placement fee between both parties. Most agencies are listed in the telephone directory, and many advertise in newspaper classified ads and in professional publications. If you decide to use one of these services, be sure you read and understand thoroughly the terms of any contracts into which you enter.

TEMPORARY PLACEMENT SERVICE

A temporary placement service is a company that provides employees to meet short-term needs. "Temps" may be needed on short notice for short periods of time, to substitute for a dental hygienist or assistant who is ill, for example, or for planned, longer periods, such as for a maternity leave or vacation. Many temporary dental care professionals have landed ideal permanent employment this way. You also get a chance to work closely with the staff and the dentist before making a permanent commitment.

DENTAL HYGIENE AND ASSISTANT SCHOOLS

Dental hygiene and assistant programs usually have a "job board" or a faculty member who keeps track of open positions, both locally and around the state. Dentists consider programs to be good sources of potential applicants, and many call or write when a position is available.

14. Get Ready for the Interview

Appearances are important in applying for a job in which you will be working with all kinds of people. Your clothes and hair should be clean and neat. If you travel to a new community for the interview, allow time to locate the office. Promptness is important, so plan to arrive on time or a few minutes early.

During the interview, ask questions about the organization, its aims and history. Observe all the details of the office for your own benefit. If you want to be considered for the position, state that you do. Write a thank-you letter in one to two days after the interview. Give any information you may not have supplied and reemphasize your interest in the position.

Be ready to repeat these steps until you have found the position and location that is right for you.

CHAPTER 8

STATUS OF DENTISTRY

Dentistry, with its associated careers, is a changing profession. As in many other scientific and health-related fields, advances in science and technology have led to new concepts of care. For example, lasers are used to remove caries (decay), and computers can be programmed to design precise crowns to fit teeth. Many types of implant devices hold crowns in place. As people take better care of their bodies, they are working harder to maintain healthy teeth.

A LOOK AHEAD

Experts predict that the occurrence of decay will continue to be reduced as emphasis on preventive dentistry is increased, and that periodontal (gum) disease will be a continuing problem that will need to be treated. Better materials are being developed to restore (fill) teeth and seal them against caries disease (decay). Studies are under way to measure the role of specific foods and how they effect the caries process that produces decay. In dental education, curriculums in dental schools are changing to respond to these changes: there is greater focus on patient care and caring. Another area of responsibility is concentration on care of special or handicapped patients and aged patients.

Dentistry is changing also because dental health is more important to more people today. More people are aware of preventive dentistry and do not visit a dentist just when problems occur. Instead, visits are made regularly for cleaning and checkups to prevent oral diseases and loss of teeth. This process of education has been aided by many dentists under the leadership of the American Dental Association and its many programs. Articles are appearing in popular magazines and newspapers stressing the importance of caring for teeth, regular dental visits, and the cosmetic appearance of teeth.

JOB OUTLOOK

Employment of dentists is expected to grow slower than the average for all occupations through the year 2006. While employment growth will provide some job opportunities, most jobs will result from the need to replace the large number of dentists projected to retire. Job prospects should be good if the number of dental school graduates does not grow significantly, thus keeping the supply of newly qualified dentists near current levels.

There is cause for some concern about the outlook, however, because the number of first-year enrollees in dental school programs has increased over enrollment in the late 1980s. If the number of enrollees continues to increase, there will be a larger pool of dentists, and job seekers may face competition.

Demand for dental care should grow substantially through 2006. As members of the baby-boom generation advance into middle age, a large number will need maintenance on complicated dental work, such as bridges. In addition, elderly people are more likely to retain their teeth than their predecessors, so they will require much more care than in the past. The younger generation will continue to need preventive check ups despite treatments such as fluoridation of the water supply, which decreases the incidence of tooth decay.

However, the employment of dentists is not expected to grow as rapidly as the demand for dental services. As their practices expand, dentists are likely to hire more dental hygienists and dental assistants to handle routine services they now perform themselves.

DENTAL INSURANCE

Dental insurance, in addition to medical insurance, is becoming more common. Currently, one hundred million Americans have this coverage. Private dental insurance payments accounted for a significant percentage of the national expenditure for dental care in 2000.

Nearly all dental plans are sold to groups such as employees of companies, members of unions and associations, and school groups. Basic dental insurance policies cover recurrent dental procedures such as examinations, cleanings, and filling of cavities. Dental insurance procedures can prevent small problems from becoming large ones.

In some insurance plans, families or individuals enroll in a Health Maintenance Organization in which they are treated at a specified facility. In these facilities, groups of dentists, hygienists, and assistants provide treatment. A patient may not always be assigned to just one practitioner but may be treated by any dentist in the group.

Increasing insurance coverage is another factor in the changing status of dentistry.

RETAIL DENTISTRY

Another indication of the changes in dentistry is a new method of service called retail dentistry—a dental facility, usually located in a retail department store or mall that offers dental service to the general public. These facilities are in a visible, convenient location, and usually are in operation the same hours as the stores around them. Although encouraged, dental appointments are not usually necessary.

The program originated in 1977 when the entire retail franchise industry was most successful. Like other franchises, the practices offered the patients convenient hours, making access to care easier. However, since their initial success, several dental franchises have closed or limited operations. As an alternative, solo and group practitioners are changing their operations to offer more convenient hours of practice and easy access for their patients.

GEOGRAPHIC LOCATIONS

The Bureau of Economic and Behavioral Research of the American Dental Association conducts regular surveys to provide information on the number and location of dentists currently practicing in the United States. The geographic sections are those defined by the United States census. In the last census, in the densely populated Middle Atlantic and east north central states, there were, respectively, 25,509 and 23,483 professionally active dentists. In the Pacific states, 22,906 dentists were in practice. The lowest numbers practiced in the mountain and east south central areas. The total number of practicing dentists in the United States was 137,817.

These figures are compiled by the American Dental Association to help individual practitioners select practice locations and identify areas that need dental services and offer opportunities for professional development. A survey of dental school graduates showing locations where they hoped to be employed indicated that graduates planned to move away from the large metropolitan districts, small towns, and rural areas toward more medium-sized locations.

WOMEN AND MINORITY GROUPS

The various positions in dentistry have been filled by men and women in traditional roles. Men have been dominant in the professional role of dentists; women have been hygienists and assistants; men have been in the majority as laboratory technicians.

However, emphasis on these roles is changing. The most dramatic change is the increased percentage of women entering the nation's dental schools. The percentage of first-year enrollment by women increased from 17.5 percent in 1979, to 33.2 percent in 1988, to close to 50 percent in 2000.

In some European countries, dentistry is a field dominated by women. For example, approximately half the dentists in Greece are women; nearly 80 percent of the dentists in Poland, Finland, and Russia are women.

The increase in the number of women entering United States dental schools can be related to the changing status of women as reflected by the increased number of women in the work force. Most dentists, including women dentists, are owners or share in the ownership of the practice in which they treat patients. Women practitioners averaged about 41.5 hours in the practice each week, with about 31.4 hours devoted to treating patients. More than 80 percent of all women dentists are younger than forty years, 73 percent were or had been married, and 49 percent were parents. About 32 percent of the women said they had taken leave for child rearing. The independence of the profession permits a more flexible schedule for family concerns for both men and women.

The roles of assistants and hygienists are no longer rigidly defined. As people in these positions assume more responsibilities and independence, the work can become more rewarding and fulfilling for both men and women. These two careers, plus that of the laboratory technician, are open to those who are qualified—regardless of gender.

Minority Students

The number of students from ethnic minority groups has steadily increased in all phases of dental training. To encourage students from minority groups to pursue dentistry as a career, the American Fund for Dental Health sponsors a program of scholarships for minority students. Students selected under this program may receive $2,000 or more for their first year of dental school. Given satisfactory progress and availability of funds, another grant may be provided to help the student in the second year.

The enrollment of minority students in dental schools has increased steadily. The percentage of black first-year students enrolled in dental schools increased from 6.4 percent in 1987–88 to 6.9 percent in 1988–89. In the ten years since, the percentage has gone up several more points. Hispanic students comprised 7.5 percent; American Indians, 0.5 percent; Asian students, 16.2 percent. Similar increases have occurred in training programs for hygienists, assistants, and laboratory technicians. In summary, there are no gender or ethnic barriers to entrance to a career in dentistry.

SPECIAL CONCERNS

As individuals and through their professional associations, dentists, hygienists, and assistants have worked to promote oral health for everyone. Large-scale programs have been started to prevent and control dental disease:

- fluoridation of community water supplies
- national dental health programs for children
- placement programs and efforts to bring dentists into the small communities
- provision of dental care for children within Medicaid and senior citizens within Medicare

However, large groups of people do not receive dental care: the poor, elderly, handicapped, homebound, and institutionalized. Today, attempts are being made to improve the opportunity for some of these people to receive dental care. These attempts are opening new possibilities for service within the dental profession.

The Poor

In some areas of the country, children are receiving oral health education and preventive services in the schools. A community effort in New York State provided and equipped a dental van in which dentists and assistants travel to treat children.

Members of the Auxiliary to the American Dental Association, a special group comprised of dental spouses, volunteer to increase the oral health of children, senior citizens, handicapped persons, and the public in general.

The Elderly

Dentures have been supplied at cost to elderly persons through programs of several dental societies. Treatment has also been offered to those who do not need dentures. Several dental groups offer reduced fees for persons sixty-five years and older.

The Handicapped

Since 1975, the National Foundation of Dentistry for the Handicapped has worked to treat the dental needs of those who are not receiving care. They have developed three programs.

The Campaign of Concern focuses on the mentally handicapped and others afflicted with developmental disabilities. It emphasizes teaching oral hygiene skills, diagnosing disease, and helping patients gain access to dental care by either arranging for their transportation to the dental office or scheduling volunteer dentists to make house calls. Since its inception in 1975, the campaign has served more than forty-five thousand people in eleven participating states. Nearly thirty-seven million people in the United States are identified as having some physical, mental, or emotional condition that limits their ability to function completely. Many of these people also have poor oral health conditions that limit their ability to speak and eat properly.

The Homebound

Dentistry for the Homebound is specifically aimed at securing dental treatment for those whose disabilities restrict them to their homes or long-term care facilities. The program includes a van with portable dental equipment for dentists. The project has been established in Denver, Chicago, Newark, Detroit, and Houston. About a thousand patients are treated every year in each city.

Volunteer Dentists

The Donated Dental Services program involves matching volunteer dentists with the indigent elderly, handicapped, mentally ill, and homeless who cannot pay for dental care. In Colorado, where the first DDS program was formed in 1985, more than five hundred patients receive an average of more than $700 free dental treatment every year. Other DDS projects are currently under way in ten other states.

These programs and others show the commitment of professionals in the dental health care field. Career opportunities are available for persons with concern who want to work with all types of special patients.

THE PROFESSIONAL IN THE COMMUNITY

Because the dental care professional is concerned about better health for everyone, he or she is likely to become involved in community projects. This involvement may be in the form of service clubs, planning boards, school boards, or any activity that contributes to the general community improvement.

Dentists, hygienists, and assistants also take part in local, state, and national meetings of dental professional associations. Local study clubs present new information or techniques. Often, the work of these organizations can lead to action within a community, such as a campaign for fluoridated water or care for a special group of patients.

In their communities, many dentists, hygienists, and assistants initiate an annual educational program for children. During the month of February, millions of schoolchildren are given dental health instruction through planned programs and activities. The slogan, "Smile America," is emphasized in schools, shopping centers, hospitals, and libraries.

Special materials—posters, calendars, buttons, bookmarks, balloons, and stickers—are developed by the American Dental Association and distributed to volunteers who plan the local projects. Announcements on radio and television are emphasized during the month. Correct methods of cleaning teeth are stressed in skits, clean-teeth contests, and puppet shows.

Much time is given by volunteers—dentists, hygienists, assistants, and others—to make these programs during Children's Dental Health Month successful.

The dental health care professional is a respected person in the community and, as such, can and does exert influence for the benefit of the public. This responsibility is one shared by leaders in the dental profession.

PROFESSIONAL ASSOCIATIONS

DENTAL ASSISTANTS

American Dental Assistants
   Association
203 N. LaSalle St., Suite 1320
Chicago, IL 60601-1210

Dental Assisting National Board,
   Inc.
676 N. Saint Clair St., Suite
   1880
Chicago, IL 60611-2927
www.dentalassisting.com

DENTAL HYGIENISTS

American Dental Hygienists'
   Association
444 N. Michigan Ave., Suite
   3400
Chicago, IL 60611
www.adha.org/

National Dental Hygienists
   Association
45 S. Idlewild St., Suite 808
Memphis, TN 38104-3983
www.adha.org

DENTISTS

Academy of Dentistry
  International
  5125 MacArthur Blvd. NW,
    Suite 50
  Washington, DC 20016-3300

Academy of Dentistry for
  Persons with Disabilities
  211 E. Chicago Ave., 5th
    Floor
  Chicago, IL 60611-2637

Academy of General Dentistry
  211 E. Chicago Ave., Suite
    1200
  Chicago, IL 60611-2637
  www.agd.org

Academy for Implants and
  Transplants
  7015 Old Keene Mill Rd.
  Springfield, VA 22150-2805

Academy of Laser Dentistry
  9629 Westview Dr., Suite 440
  Coral Springs, FL 33076-2513
  www.laserdentistry.org

Academy of Operative Dentistry
  P.O. Box 177
  Menomonie, WI 54751-0177

Academy of Prosthodontics
  4830 V St. NW
  Washington, DC 20007-1511

Academy for Sports Dentistry
  Dr. William Olin
  Otolaryngology Dept.
  University Hospital & Clinics
  Iowa City, IA 52242
  www.sportsdentistry.com

Alliance of the American Dental
  Association
  211 E. Chicago Ave., 5th
    Floor
  Chicago, IL 60611-2637
  www.allianceada.org

American Academy of Cosmetic
  Dentistry
  2810 Walton Commons W,
    Suite 200
  Madison, WI 53718-3900
  www.aacd.com

American Academy of Dental
  Electrosurgery
  15 W. 81st St.
  New York, NY 10024-6022

American Academy of Dental
  Group Practice
  2525 E. Arizona Biltmore
    Circle, Suite 127
  Phoenix, AZ 85016-2146
  www.aadgp.org

American Academy of Esthetic
Dentistry
401 N. Michigan Ave., Suite
2400
Chicago, IL 60611-4255

American Academy of Fixed
Prosthodontics
P.O. Box 1409
1930 Sea Way
Bodega Bay, CA 94923

American Academy of
Gnathologic Orthopedics
2651 Oak Grove Rd.
Walnut Creek, CA 94598-
3627
www.aago.com

American Academy of Implant
Dentistry
211 E. Chicago Ave., Suite
750
Chicago, IL 60611-2637
www.aaid-implant.org

American Academy of Implant
Prosthodontics
760 Whitehall Way
Roswell, GA 30076-1363

American Academy of
Orthodontics for the
General Practitioner
920 Bascom Hill Dr.
Baraboo, WI 53913-1281

American Academy of Pediatric
Dentistry
211 E. Chicago Ave., Suite
700
Chicago, IL 60611-2637
www.aapd.org

American Academy of
Periodontology
737 N. Michigan Ave., Suite
800
Chicago, IL 60611-2615
www.perio.org

American Academy of
Restorative Dentistry
1184 College Ave.
Elko, NV 89801-3424

American Association for Dental
Research
1619 Duke St.
Alexandria, VA 22314-3406
www.iadr.com

American Association of Dental
Schools
1625 Massachusetts Ave. NW,
Suite 600
Washington, DC 20036
www.aads.jhu.edu

American Association of
Endodontists
211 E. Chicago Ave., Suite
1100
Chicago, IL 60611-2637
www.aae.org

American Association of
    Hospital Dentists
    211 E. Chicago Ave., 5th
      Floor
    Chicago, IL 60611-2637

American Association of Oral
    and Maxillofacial Surgeons
    9700 Bryn Mawr Ave.
    Rosemont, IL 60018-5701
    www.aaoms.org

American Association of
    Orthodontists
    401 N. Lindbergh Blvd.
    Saint Louis, MO 63141-7839
    www.aaortho.org

American Association of Public
    Health Dentistry
    National Office
    3760 SW. Lyle Ct.
    Portland, OR 97221-3963
    www.pitt.edu

American Dental Association
    211 E. Chicago Ave.
    Chicago, IL 60611
    www.ada.org

American Student Dental
    Association
    211 E. Chicago Ave., Suite
      1160
    Chicago, IL 60611-2637
    www.asdanet.org

National Dental Association
    3517 16th St. NW
    Washington, DC 20010-3041

LABORATORY TECHNICIANS

National Association of Dental
    Laboratories
    8201 Greensboro Dr., Suite
      300
    McLean, VA 22102-3810
    www.nald.org

DENTAL SCHOOLS

U.S. SCHOOLS

Alabama

University of Alabama
  School of Dentistry
  1919 7th Ave. S
  Birmingham, AL 35294

California

Loma Linda University
  School of Dentistry
  Loma Linda, CA 92350

University of California, Los
    Angeles
  School of Dentistry
  Los Angeles, CA 90095-1668

University of California
  School of Dentistry
  513 Parnassus Ave., S-630
  San Francisco, CA 94143

University of the Pacific
  School of Dentistry
  2155 Webster St.
  San Francisco, CA 94115

University of Southern
    California
  School of Dentistry, Rm. 203
  University Park–Mc 0641
  Los Angeles, CA 90089-0641

Colorado

University of Colorado
  Medical Center School of
    Dentistry
  4200 E. 9th Ave., Box A095
  Denver, CO 80262

Connecticut

The University of Connecticut
  School of Dental Medicine
  263 Farmington Ave.
  Farmington, CT 06032

District of Columbia

Howard University
  College of Dentistry
  600 W St. NW
  Washington, DC 20059

Florida

Nova Southeastern University
  College of Dental Medicine
  3200 S. University Dr.
  Fort Lauderdale, FL 33328

University of Florida
  College of Dentistry
  P.O. Box 100405
  Gainesville, FL 32610-0405

Georgia

Medical College of Georgia
  School of Dentistry
  1459 Laney Walker Blvd.
  Augusta, GA 30912-0200

Illinois

Northwestern University
  Office of the Dean
  Dental School
  240 E. Huron St.
  Chicago, IL 60611

Southern Illinois University
  School of Dental Medicine
    Building 273
  2800 College Ave., Rm. 2300
  Alton, IL 62002

University of Illinois at Chicago
  College of Dentistry
  801 S. Paulina St.
  Chicago, IL 60612

Indiana

Indiana University
  School of Dentistry
  1121 W. Michigan St.
  Indianapolis, IN 46202

Iowa

The University of Iowa
  College of Dentistry
  Dental Building
  Iowa City, IA 52242

Kentucky

University of Kentucky
  College of Dentistry
  800 Rose St.– Medical Center
  Lexington, KY 40536-0084

University of Louisville
  School of Dentistry
  Health Sciences Center
  Louisville, KY 40292

Louisiana

Louisiana State University
  School of Dentistry
  1100 Florida Ave., Bldg. 101
  New Orleans, LA 70119

Maryland

University of Maryland
  Baltimore College of Dental
    Surgery
  666 W. Baltimore St.
  Baltimore, MD 21201

Massachusetts

Boston University
  Henry M. Goldman School of
    Dental Medicine
  100 E. Newton St.
  Boston, MA 02118

Harvard School of Dental
    Medicine
  188 Longwood Ave.
  Boston, MA 02115

Tufts University
  School of Dental Medicine
  1 Kneeland St.
  Boston, MA 02111

Michigan

University of Detroit Mercy
  School of Dentistry
  8200 W. Outer Dr.
  P.O. Box 98
  Detroit, MI 48219-0900

University of Michigan
  School of Dentistry
  1234 Dental Bldg.
  Ann Arbor, MI 48109-1078

Minnesota

University of Minnesota
  School of Dentistry
  515 SE. Delaware St.
  Minneapolis, MN 55455

Mississippi

University of Mississippi
  School of Dentistry–Medical
    Center
  2500 N. State St.
  Jackson, MS 39216-4505

Missouri

University of Missouri-Kansas
    City
  School of Dentistry
  650 E. 25th St.
  Kansas City, MO 64108

Nebraska

Creighton University
  School of Dentistry
  2500 California St.
  Omaha, NE 68178

University of Nebraska
  Medical Center
  College of Dentistry
  40th & Holdrege Sts.
  Lincoln, NE 68583-0740

New Jersey

University of Medicine &
    Dentistry
  New Jersey Dental School
  110 Bergen St.
  Newark, NJ 07103-2425

New York

Columbia University
School of Dental & Oral
Surgery
630 W. 168th St.
New York, NY 10032

New York University
College of Dentistry
345 E. 24th St.
New York, NY 10010

State University of New York
School of Dental Medicine
325 Squire Hall
Buffalo, NY 14214

State University of New York
School of Dental Medicine
Rockland Hall
Stony Brook, NY 11794-8700

North Carolina

University of North Carolina
School of Dentistry
104 Brauer Hall, 211 H
Chapel Hill, NC 27599-7450

Ohio

Case Western Reserve
University
School of Dentistry
2123 Abington Rd.
Cleveland, OH 44106

Ohio State University
College of Dentistry
305 W. 12th Ave.
Columbus, OH 43210

Oklahoma

University of Oklahoma, Health
Science Center College of
Dentistry
P.O. Box 26901
Oklahoma City, OK 73190

Oregon

The Oregon Health Science
University
School of Dentistry– Sam
Jackson Pk.
611 SW. Campus Dr.
Portland, OR 97201

Pennsylvania

Temple University
School of Dentistry
3223 N. Broad St.
Philadelphia, PA 19140

University of Pennsylvania
School of Dental Medicine
4001 W. Spruce St.
Philadelphia, PA 19104

University of Pittsburgh
School of Dental Medicine
3501 Terrace St.
Pittsburgh, PA 15261

Puerto Rico

University of Puerto Rico
School of Dentistry
Medical Sciences Campus
P.O. BOX 365067
San Juan, PR 00936-5067

South Carolina

Medical University of South
    Carolina
    College of Dental Medicine
    171 Ashley Ave.
    Charleston, SC 29425

Tennessee

Meharry Medical College
    School of Dentistry
    1005 18th Ave. N
    Nashville, TN 37208

University of Tennessee
    College of Dentistry
    875 Union Ave.
    Memphis, TN 38163

Texas

Texas A&M University System
    Baylor College of Dentistry
    P.O. Box 660677
    Dallas, TX 75266-0677

The University of Texas
    Health Science Center–Dental
    Branch
    6516 John Freeman Ave.
    Houston, TX 77030

The University of Texas
    Health Science Center–Dental
    School
    7703 Floyd Curl Dr.
    San Antonio, TX 78284-7914

Virginia

Virginia Commonwealth
    University
    VCU–School of Dentistry
    P.O. Box 980566
    Richmond, VA 23298-0566

Washington

University of Washington
    School of Dentistry
    Health Science Bldg. Sc-62
    Seattle, WA 98195

West Virginia

West Virginia University
    School of Dentistry
    P.O. Box 9400
    Morgantown, WV
    26506-9400

Wisconsin

Marquette University
    School of Dentistry
    P.O. Box 1881
    Milwaukee, WI 53201

CANADIAN SCHOOLS

Dalhousie University
    Faculty of Dentistry
    5981 University Ave.
    Halifax, Nova Scotia B3H 3J5

Ecole De Medecine Dentaire
    Universite Laval
    Ste-Foy, Quebec GIK 7P4

University of Alberta
    Faculty of Medicine and Oral
        Health Sciences
    Room 3036, Dent/Pharma
        Bldg.
    Edmonton, Alberta T6G 2N8

University of British Columbia
    Faculty of Dentistry
    350-2194 Health Sciences
        Mall
    Vancouver, British Columbia
        V6T 1Z3

University of Manitoba
    Faculty of Dentistry
    780 Bannatyne Ave., Rm.
        D113
    Winnepeg, Manitoba R3E
        0W2

Universite De Montreal
    School of Dental Medicine
    C.P. 6128 Succursale A
    Montreal, Quebec H3C 3J7

University of Saskatchewan
    College of Dentistry
    107 Wiggins Rd., Rm. B526
    Saskatoon, Saskatchewan S7N
        5E5

University of Toronto
    Faculty of Dentistry
    124 Edward St.
    Toronto, Ontario M5G 1G6

University of Western Ontario
    Faculty of Medicine and
        Dentistry
    1151 Richmond St.
    London, Ontario N6A 5C1

ACCREDITED DENTAL HYGIENE PROGRAMS

U.S. SCHOOLS

Alabama

Council Trenholm State
  1225 Air Base Blvd.
  Montgomery, AL 36108

Wallace State Community
  College
  P.O. Box 2000
  Hanceville, AL 35077-2000

Alaska

University of Alaska Anchorage
  Dental Programs–AHS Bldg.
  3211 Providence Dr.
  Anchorage, AK 99508-4670

Arizona

Northern Arizona University
  Department of Dental
  Hygiene
  P.O. Box 15065
  Flagstaff, AZ 86011

Phoenix College
  1202 W. Thomas Rd.
  Phoenix, AZ 85013

Pima County Community
  College
  2202 W. Anklam Rd.
  Tucson, AZ 85709

Rio Salado College
  2323 W. 14th St.
  Tempe, AZ 85281-6950

Arkansas

University of Arkansas
Medical Sciences
4301 W. Markham St.
Little Rock, AR 72205

Westark College
5210 Grand Ave.
P.O. Box 3649
Ft. Smith, AR 72913-3649

California

Cabrillo College
6500 Soquel Dr.
Aptos, CA 95003

Cerritos College
11110 E. Alondra Blvd.
Norwalk, CA 90650

Chabot College
25555 Hesperian Blvd.
Hayward, CA 94545

Cypress College
9200 Valley View St.
Cypress, CA 90630

Diablo Valley College
321 Golf Club Rd.
Pleasant Hill, CA 94523

Foothill College
12345 El Monte Rd.
Los Altos Hills, CA 94022

Fresno City College
1101 E. University
Fresno, CA 93741

Loma Linda University
School of Dentistry
Loma Linda, CA 92350

Oxnard College
4000 S. Rose Ave.
Oxnard, CA 93033-6699

Pasadena City College
1570 E. Colorado Blvd.
Pasadena, CA 91106

Sacramento City College
3835 Freeport Blvd.
Sacramento, CA 95822

San Joaquin Valley College
8400 W. Mineral King
Visalia, CA 93291

Santa Rosa Junior College
1501 Mendocino Ave.
Santa Rosa, CA 95401-4395

Taft College
29 Emmons Park Dr.
Box 1437
Taft, CA 93268

University of California
School of Dentistry-Division
of Dental Hygiene
P.O. Box 0754
San Francisco, CA 94143

University of Southern
California
Department of Dental
Hygiene
University Park–MC0641,
Rm. 4304
Los Angeles, CA 90089-0641

West Los Angeles College
4800 Freshman Dr.
Culver City, CA 90230

Colorado

Colorado Northwestern
Community College
500 Kennedy Dr.
Rangely, CO 81648

Community College of Denver
960 Xanthia St.
Denver, CO 80220

Pueblo Community College–DH
900 W. Orman Ave.
Pueblo, CO 81004

University of Colorado
4200 E. 9th Ave.
Box C284
Denver, CO 80262

Connecticut

Tunxis Community–Tech.
College
271 Scott Swamp Rd.
Farmington, CT 06032-3187

University of Bridgeport
Fones School of Dental
Hygiene
30 Hazel St.
Bridgeport, CT 06604

University of New Haven
Department of Dental
Hygiene
300 Orange Ave.
West Haven, CT 06516

Delaware

Delaware Tech. & Community
College
333 Shipley St.
Wilmington, DE 19801

District of Columbia

Howard University
College of Dentistry
600 W St. NW
Washington, DC 20059

Florida

Brevard Community College
1519 Clearlake Rd.
Cocoa, FL 32922

Broward Community College
3501 SW. Davie Rd.
Ft. Lauderdale, FL 333141

Daytona Beach Community
    College
1200 International Speedway
Daytona Beach, FL 32114

Edison Community College
8099 College Parkway SW
Ft. Myers, FL 33906-6210

Florida Community College
    Jacksonville
4501 Capper Rd.
Jacksonville, FL 32218

Gulf Coast Community College
5230 W. Highway 98
Panama City, FL 32401-10411

Indian River Community
    College
3209 Virginia Ave.
Ft. Pierce, FL 34981-5599

Manatee Community College
5840 26th St. W
Bradenton, FL 34207

Miami–Dade Community
    College-Medical Center
950 NW. 20th St.
Miami, FL 33127

Palm Beach Community College
4200 Congress Ave.
Lake Worth, FL 33461

Pasco–Hernando Community
    College
10230 Ridge Rd.
New Port Richey, FL 34654-
    5199

Pensacola Junior College
5555 W. Highway 98
Pensacola, FL 32507

Santa Fe Community College
3000 NW. 83rd St.
Gainesville, FL 32606

St. Petersburg Junior College
P.O. Box 13489
St. Petersburg, FL 33733

Tallahassee Community
    College–DH
444 Appleyard Dr.
Tallahassee, FL 32304

Valencia Community College
1800 S. Kirkman Rd.
Orlando, FL 32811

Georgia

Armstrong Atlantic State Univ.
    Department of Dental
    Hygiene
11935 Abercorn St.
Savannah, GA 31419-1997

Athens Area Technical Institute
800 U.S. Highway 29 N
Athens, GA 30601-1500

Carroll Technical Institute
4600 Timber Ridge Dr.
Douglasville, GA 30135

Clayton College and State
   University
   Department of Dental
      Hygiene
   5900 Lee St.
   Morrow, GA 30260

Columbus Technical Institute
   928 45th St.
   Columbus, GA 31904-6572

Darton College
   2400 Gillionville Rd.
   Albany, GA 31707

Floyd College
   809 Keelway Dr.
   Rome, GA 30165

Georgia Perimeter College
   2101 Womack Rd.
   Dunwoody, GA 30338-4497

Lanier Tech./Gainesville College
   P.O. Box 58
   Oakwood, GA 30566

Macon State College
   100 College Station Drive
   Macon, GA 31297

Medical College of Georgia
   Department of Dental
      Hygiene
   1120 15th St., AD-311
   Augusta, GA 30912

Valdosta State University/
   Technical College
   P.O. Box 928-4089
   Val Tech Rd.
   Valdosta, GA 31603-0928

Hawaii

University of Hawaii
   2445 Campus Rd., Rm. 200-B
   Honolulu, HI 96822

University of Hawaii at Manoa
   Department of Dental
      Hygiene
   2445 Campus Rd.
   Hemenway Hall, Rm. 200B
   Honolulu, HI 96822

Idaho

American Institute of Health
      Technologies
   6600 Emerald
   Boise, ID 83704

Idaho State University
   741 S. 8th St.
   Pocatello, ID 83209

Illinois

Illinois Central College
   201 SW. Adams St.
   Peoria, IL 61635-0001

Kennedy–King College
   6800 S. Wentworth Ave.
   Chicago, IL 60621

Lake Land College
5001 Lake Land Blvd.
Mattoon, IL 61938-9366

Lewis & Clark Community
College
5800 Godfrey Rd.
Godfrey, IL 62035

Parkland College
2400 W. Bradley
Champaign, IL 61821

Prairie State College
202 S. Halsted
Chicago Heights, IL 60411

Southern Illinois University
Dental Hygiene Program
Department of Health Care
Professions
College of Applied Sciences
and Arts
Mail Code 6615
Carbondale, IL 62901-6615

William Rainey Harper College
1200 W. Algonquin Rd.
Palatine, IL 60067

Indiana

Indiana University Med. Cntr.
Department of Periodontics
and Allied Dental Programs
School of Dentistry
1121 W. Michigan
Indianapolis, IN 46202

Indiana University Northwest
Department of Dental
Hygiene
School of Dentistry
3223 Broadway
Gary, IN 46409

Indiana University–Purdue at
Fort Wayne
Department of Dental
Hygiene
2101 Coliseum Blvd. E.
Fort Wayne, IN 46805-1499

Indiana University/South Bend
Department of Dental
Hygiene
1700 Mishawaka Ave.
Box 7111
South Bend, IN 46634

University of Southern Indiana
Department of Dental
Hygiene
8600 University Blvd.
Evansville, IN 47712

Iowa

Des Moines Area Community
College
2006 Ankeny Blvd.
Ankeny, IA 50021

Hawkeye Community College
1501 E. Orange Rd., Box 8015
Waterloo, IA 50704

Iowa Western Community
  College
  2700 College Rd., Box 4C
  Council Bluffs, IA 51502-
  3004

Kansas

Johnson County Community
  College
  12345 College Blvd.
  Overland Park, KS 66210-
  1299

Northcentral–Colby Community
  College
  1255 S. Range
  Colby, KS 67701

Wichita State University
  Department of Dental
  Hygiene
  1845 N. Fairmount
  Wichita, KS 67260-0144

Kentucky

Henderson Community College
  2660 S. Green St.
  Henderson, KY 42420

Lexington Community College
  Cooper Dr.–Oswald Bldg.
  Lexington, KY 40506

Prestonsburg Community
  College
  One Bert T. Combs Dr.
  Prestonsburg, KY 41653

University of Louisville
  Department of Dental
  Hygiene
  School of Dentistry
  Health Sciences Center
  Louisville, KY 40292

Western Kentucky University
  Department of Allied Health
  Program of Dental Hygiene
  Academic Complex–Rm. 207
  Bowling Green, KY 42101

Louisiana

Louisiana State University
  School of Dentistry
  Department of Dental
  Hygiene
  1100 Florida Ave.
  New Orleans, LA 70119

Northeast Louisiana University
  School of Allied Sciences
  Dental Hygiene Program
  700 University Ave.
  Monroe, LA 71209

Southern University
  3050 Martin Luther King, Jr.
  Shreveport, LA 71107

Maine

University College of Bangor
Lincoln Hall
29 Texas Ave.
Bangor, ME 04401-4324

University of New England
Westbrook College Campus
Dental Hygiene Program
716 Stevens Ave.
Portland, ME 04103

Maryland

Allegany Community College
12401 Willowbrook Rd. SE
Cumberland, MD 21502-2596

Baltimore City Community
College
2901 Liberty Heights Ave.
Baltimore, MD 21215

University of Maryland
Department of Dental
Hygiene
666 W. Baltimore St.,
Rm. 3-G-31
Baltimore, MD 21201-1586

Massachusetts

Bristol Community College
777 Elsbree St.
Fall River, MA 02720

Cape Cod Community College
Route 132
West Barnstable, MA 02668

Forsyth School for Dental
Hygienists
Department of Dental
Hygiene
140 The Fenway
Boston, MA 02115

Middlesex Community College
33 Kearney Square
Lowell, MA 01852

Mount Ida College
777 Dedham St.
Newton Centre, MA 02159

Quinsigamond Community
College
670 W. Boylston St.
Worcester, MA 01606

Springfield Technical
Community College
One Armory Square
Springfield, MA 01105

Michigan

Baker College of Port Huron
3403 Lapeer Rd.
Port Huron, MI 48060

Ferris State University
  College of Allied Health
    Sciences
  Dental Hygiene Program
  200 Ferris Dr.
  Big Rapids, MI 49307-2740

Grand Rapids Community
    College
  143 Bostwick St. NE
  Grand Rapids, MI 49503

Kalamazoo Valley Community
    College
  6767 West O Ave., Box 4070
  Kalamazoo, MI 49003-4070

Kellogg Community College
  450 North Ave.
  Battle Creek, MI 49016

Lansing Community College
  P.O. Box 40010
  Lansing, MI 48901-7210

Mott Community College
  1401 E. Court St.
  Flint, MI 48503

Oakland Community College
  7350 Cooley Lake Rd.
  Waterford, MI 48327

University of Detroit Mercy
  Department of Dental
    Hygiene
  8200 W. Outer Dr.
  Detroit, MI 48219

University of Michigan
  Department of Dental
    Hygiene
  School of Dentistry
  1011 N. University
  Ann Arbor, MI 48109-1078

Wayne County Community
    College
  8551 Greenfield, Rm. 310
  Detroit, MI 48228

Minnesota

Century College
  3300 Century Ave. N
  White Bear Lake, MN 55110

Lake Superior College
  2101 Trinity Rd.
  Duluth, MN 55811

Minnesota State University-
    Mankato
  Box 8400
  P.O. Box 81
  Mankato, MN 56002-8400

Normandale Community
    College
  9700 France Ave. S
  Bloomington, MN 55431

Northwest Technical
    College–Hygeine
  1900 28th Ave. S
  Moorhead, MN 56560-4899

Rochester Community &
    Technical College
851 30th Ave. SE
Rochester, MN 55904

St. Cloud Technical College
1540 Northway Dr.
St. Cloud, MN 56303-1240

University of Minnesota
9-436 Moos Tower
Minneapolis, MN 55455

Mississippi

Meridian Community College
910 Highway 19 N
Meridian, MS 39307

Northeast Mississippi
    Community College
Booneville, MS 38829

Pearl River Community College
5448 U.S. Highway 49 S
Hattiesburg, MS 39401

University of Mississippi
    Medical Center
Department of Dental
    Hygiene
SHRP
2500 N. State St.
Jackson, MS 39216-4505

Missouri

Missouri Southern State College
Newman & Duquesne Rds.
Joplin, MO 64801

St. Louis Community College-
    Forest Pk.
5600 Oakland Ave.
St. Louis, MO 63110-1393

University of Missouri–Kansas
    City
School of Dentistry
Division of Dental Hygiene
650 E. 25th
Kansas City, MO 64108-2795

Nebraska

Central Community College
P.O. Box 1024
Hastings, NE 68902-1024

University of Nebraska Medical
    Center
Department of Dental
    Hygiene
College of Dentistry
40th and Holdrege
Lincoln, NE 68583-0740

Nevada

Community College of Southern
    Nevada
    6375 W. Charleston Blvd.
    Las Vegas, NV 89102

New Hampshire

New Hampshire Technical
    Institute
    11 Institute Dr.
    Concord, NH 03301-7412

New Jersey

Bergen Community College
    400 Paramus Rd.
    Paramus, NJ 07652

Camden County College
    P.O. Box 200
    Blackwood, NJ 08012

Middlesex County College
    2600 Woodbridge Ave., Box
        3050
    Edison, NJ 08818

University of Medicine &
    Dentistry of New Jersey
    School of Health Related
        Professions
    1776 Rariton Rd., Rm. 425
    Scotch Plains, NJ 07076

New Mexico

University of New Mexico
    Division of Dental Hygiene
    2320 Tucker NE
    Albuquerque, NM 87131-
        1391

New York

Broome Community College
    P.O. Box 1017
    Binghamton, NY 13902

Dental Hygiene Program
    345 E. 24th St., Rm. 880W
    New York, NY 10010

Erie Community College–North
    Campus
    6205 Main St.
    Williamsville, NY 14221-
        7095

Eugenio Maria De Hostos
    College
    475 Grand Concourse
    Bronx, NY 10451

Hudson Valley Community
    College
    80 Vandenburgh Ave.
    Troy, NY 12180

Monroe Community College
    1000 E. Henrietta Rd.
    Rochester, NY 14623-5780

New York City Tech. College
300 Jay St.
Brooklyn, NY 11201

New York University Dental
Center
State University of New York
Route 110
Farmingdale, NY 11735

New York University Dental
Center
345 E. 24th St.
New York, NY 10010

Onondaga Community College
Route 173
Syracuse, NY 13215

Orange County Community
College
115 South St.
Middletown, NY 10940

North Carolina

Asheville–Buncombe Tech.
340 Victoria Rd.
Asheville, NC 28801

Cape Fear Community College
411 N. Front St.
Wilmington, NC 28401-3993

Catawba Valley Comm. College
2550 Highway 70
Sehickory, NC 28602

Central Piedmont Community
College
1201 Elizabeth Ave.–Kings
Dr.
Charlotte, NC 28204

Coastal Carolina Community
College
444 Western Blvd.
Jacksonville, NC 28540

Fayetteville Technical
Community College
2201 Hull Rd.
P.O. Box 35236
Fayetteville, NC 28303

Guilford Technical Community
College
P.O. Box 309
Jamestown, NC 27282

University of North Carolina
Degree–Completion Dental
Hygiene Program
367 Old Dental Bldg., CB
#7450
Chapel Hill, NC 27599-7450

Wayne Community College
Caller Box 8002
Goldsboro, NC 27530

North Dakota

North Dakota State College of
    Science
Wahpeton, ND 58076

Ohio

Cuyahoga Community College
    2900 Community College
    Ave.
    Cleveland, OH 44115

Lakeland Community College
    7700 Clocktower Dr.
    Kirtland, OH 44094

Lima Technical College
    4240 Campus Dr.
    Lima, OH 45804

Lorain County Community
    College
    Division of Allied Health and
    Nursing
    1005 N. Abbe Rd.
    Elyria, OH 44035-1691

Ohio State University
    Dental Hygiene, Section of
    Primary Care
    3082 Postle Hall
    305 W. 12th Ave.
    Columbus, OH 43210

Owens State Community Coll.
    P.O. Box 10000
    Toledo, OH 43699

Shawnee State University
    940 Second St.
    Portsmouth, OH 45662

Sinclair Community College
    444 W. Third St.
    Dayton, OH 45402

Stark State College of
    Technology
    6200 Frank Ave. NW
    Canton, OH 44720-7299

University of Cincinnati/
    Raymond Walters College
    9555 Plainfield Rd.
    Cincinnati, OH 45236

Youngstown State University
    Department of Health
    Professions
    Dental Hygiene Program
    One University Plaza
    Youngstown, OH 44555

Oklahoma

Rose State College
    6420 SE. 15th St.
    Midwest City, OK 73110

Tulsa Community College
    909 S. Boston Ave.
    Tulsa, OK 74119-2094

University of Oklahoma–Health
 Science Center
P.O. Box 26901
Oklahoma City, OK 73190

Oregon

Lane Community College
4000 E. 30th
Eugene, OR 97405

Mt. Hood Community College
26000 SE. Stark St.
Gresham, OR 97030

Oregon Health Sciences
 University
611 SW. Campus Dr.
Portland, OR 97201

Oregon Institute of Technology
Dental Hygiene Program
3201 Campus Dr.
Klamath Falls, OR 97601-
 8801

Portland Community College
P.O. Box 19000
Portland, OR 97280-0990

Pennsylvania

Community College of
 Philadelphia
1700 Spring Garden St.
Philadelphia, PA 19130

Harcum College
750 Montgomery Ave.
Bryn Mawr, PA 19010

Harrisburg Area Community
 College
One Hacc Dr.
Harrisburg, PA 17110-2999

Luzerne County Community
 College
1333 S. Prospect St.
Nanticoke, PA 18634-3899

Manor Junior College–DH
700 Fox Chase Rd.
Jenkintown, PA 19046-3399

Montgomery County
 Community College
340 Dekalb Pike
P.O. Box 400
Blue Bell, PA 19422-0758

Northampton County
 Community College
3835 Green Pond Rd.
Bethlehem, PA 18017

Pennsylvania College of
 Technology
Health Sciences Division
Dental Hygiene Program
One College Ave., ATHS#21
Williamsport, PA 17701-5799

University of Pittsburgh
  Dental Hygiene Program
  School of Dental Medicine
  B-23 Salk Hall
  Pittsburgh, PA 15261

Westmoreland County
    Community College
  400 Armbrust Rd.
  Youngwood, PA 15697-1895

Puerto Rico

University of Puerto Rico
  1st Fl.–Academic Affairs
    Office
  San Juan, PR 00936-5067

Rhode Island

Community College of Rhode
    Island
  Louisquisset Pike
  Lincoln, RI 02865

University of Rhode Island
  Department of Dental
    Hygiene
  8 Washburn Hall
  80 Upper College Rd., Suite 1
  Kingston, RI 02881

South Carolina

Florence-Darlington Technical
    College
  P.O. Box 100548
  Florence, SC 29501-0548

Greenville Technical College
  Department of Dental
    Hygiene
  P.O. Box 5616
  Greenville, SC 29606-5616

Horry–Georgetown Technical
    College
  2050 Highway 501 E, Box
    261966
  Conway, SC 29528-6066

Midlands Technical College
  Department of Dental
    Hygiene
  P.O. Box 2408
  Columbia, SC 29202

Trident Technical College
  P.O. Box 118067
  Charleston, SC 29423-8067

York Technical College
  452 S. Anderson Rd.
  Rock Hill, SC 29730

South Dakota

University of South Dakota
  Department of Dental
    Hygiene
  120 East Hall
  414 E. Clark St.
  Vermillion, SD 57069

Tennessee

Chattanooga State Technical
Community College
4501 Amnicola Highway
Chattanooga, TN 37406-1097

East Tennessee State University
P.O. Box 70690
Johnson City, TN 37614-0690

Roane State Community College
728 Emory Valley Rd.
Oak Ridge, TN 37830

Tennessee State University
Meharry Medical College
Dept. of Dental Hygiene
3500 John A. Merritt Blvd.
P.O. Box 358
Nashville, TN 37203-1561

University of Tennessee
Department of Dental
Hygiene
822 Beale St., Rm. 321 E
Memphis, TN 38163

Texas

Amarillo College–Allied Health
Div.
P.O. Box 447
Amarillo, TX 79178

Blinn College
301 Post Office St.
Bryan, TX 77802

Coastal Bend College
3800 Charco Rd.
Beeville, TX 78102

Collin County Community
College
2200 W. University Dr.
McKinney, TX 75069-8001

Del Mar College
Baldwin & Ayers Sts.
Corpus Christi, TX 78404

El Paso Community College
P.O. Box 20500
El Paso, TX 79998

Howard College
1001 Birdwell Lane
Big Spring, TX 79720

Lamar University
Department of Dental
Hygiene
P.O. Box 10061
Beaumont, TX 77710

Midwestern State University
3410 Taft
Wichita Falls, TX 76308-2099

Tarrant County Jr. College
828 Harwood Rd.
Hurst, TX 76054

Temple College
2600 S. First St.
Temple, TX 76504-7435

Texas A&M University, Baylor
College
P.O. Box 660677
Dallas, TX 75266-0677

Texas State Tech. College
2424 Boxwood
Harlingen, TX 78550-3697

Texas Woman's University
Department of Dental
Hygiene
P.O. Box 425796
Denton, TX 76204

Tyler Junior College
P.O. Box 9020
Tyler, TX 75711

University of Texas Dental
Branch
P.O. Box 20068
Houston, TX 77225-0068

University of Texas Health
Science Center at San
Antonio
Department of Dental
Hygiene
7703 Floyd Curl Dr.
San Antonio, TX 78284-7904

Wharton County Jr. College
911 Boling Highway
Wharton, TX 77488

Utah

Dixie College
225 S. 700 E
St. George, UT 84770

Salt Lake Community College
4600 S. Redwood Rd.
Box 30808
Salt Lake City, UT 84130-
0808

Utah Valley State College
800 W. 1200 S
Orem, UT 84058

Weber State University
3920 University Circle
Ogden, UT 84408-3920

Vermont

University of Vermont
Rowell Building, Rm. 002
Burlington, VT 05405

Virginia

Northern Virginia Community
College
8333 Little River Turnpike
Annandale, VA 22003

Old Dominion University
College of Health Sciences
Hirshfield School of Dental
Hygiene
Hampton & 46th
Norfolk, VA 23529-0499

Virginia Commonwealth
University
Division of Dental Hygiene
Box 980566
Richmond, VA 23298

Virginia Western Community
College
3095 Colonial Ave. SW
Roanoke, VA 24038

Wytheville Community College
1000 E. Main St.
Wytheville, VA 24382

Washington

Clark College
1800 E. McLoughlin Blvd.
Vancouver, WA 98663

Eastern Washington University
Paulsen Building, Rm. 252
Spokane, WA 99201

Pierce College
9401 Farwest Dr. SW
Tacoma, WA 98498

Shoreline Community College
16101 Greenwood Ave.
North Seattle, WA 98133

University of Washington
School of Dentistry
Dental Hygiene Program
Box 357475
Seattle, WA 98195-7475

Yakima Valley Community
College
16th Ave., Nob Hill Blvd.
Yakima, WA 98907

West Virginia

West Liberty State College
Department of Dental
Hygiene
West Liberty, WV 26074

West Virginia University
Department of Dental
Hygiene
Health Sciences North
P.O. Box 9425
Morgantown, WV 26506-
9425

West Virginia University
Institute of Technology
Montgomery, WV 25136

Wisconsin

Madison Area Technical College
  3550 Anderson St., Rm. 300f
  Madison, WI 53704

Marquette University
  Department of Dental
    Hygiene
  College of Health Sciences
  P.O. Box 1881
  Milwaukee, WI 53201-1881

Milwaukee Area Technical
    College
  700 W. State St.
  Milwaukee, WI 53233

Northcentral Technical College
  1000 Campus Dr.
  Wausau, WI 54401

Northeast Wisconsin Technical
    College
  2740 W. Mason St.
  P.O. Box 19042
  Green Bay, WI 54307-9042

Waukesha County Technical
    College
  800 Main St.
  Pewaukee, WI 53072

Wyoming

Laramie County Community
    College
  1400 E. College Dr.
  Cheyenne, WY 82007

Sheridan College
  Department of Dental
    Hygiene
  P.O. Box 1500
  3059 Coffeen Ave.
  Sheridan, WY 82801

CANADIAN SCHOOLS

Algonquin College
  1385 Woodroffe Ave.
  Nepean, Ontario K2G 1V8

Cambrian College
  1400 Barrydowne Rd.
  Sudbury, Ontario P3A 3V8

Camosun College
  3100 Foul Bay Rd.
  Victoria, British Columbia
    V8P 4X8

Canadore College of Applied
    Arts
P.O. Box 5001
North Bay, Ontario P1B 8K9

Cegep de Chicoutimi
534, Rue Jacques-Cartier Est
Chicoutimi, Quebec G7H 1Z6

Cegep St.–Hyacinthe
300, Rue Boulle
St. Hyacinthe, Quebec J2S
1H9

Cegep de Trois–Rivieres
3500, Rue de Courval, Cp 97
Trois-Rivieres, Quebec G9A
5E6

La Cite Collegiale
807 Promenade de L'aviation
Ottawa, Ontario K1K 4R3

College Boreal
21, Boul. Lasalle
Sudbury, Ontario P3A 6B1

College Edouard–Montpetit
945, Chemin de Chambly
Longueuil, Quebec J4H 3M6

College Francois-Xavier-
    Garneau
1660, Boul. de L'entente
Sillery, Quebec G1S 4S3

College de L'outaouais
333, Boul. Cite des Juenes
Hull, Quebec J8Y 6M5

College Maisonneuve
3800 Est, Rue Sherbrooke
Montreal, Quebec H1X 2A2

College of New Caledonia
3330-22nd Ave.
Prince George, British
    Columbia V2N 1P8

Confederation College
P.O. Box 398
Thunder Bay, Ontario P7C
4W1

Dalhousie University
5981 University Ave.
Halifax, Nova Scotia B3H 3J5

Durham College
P.O. Box 385
Oshawa, Ontario L1H 7L7

Fanshawe College
P.O. Box 4005
London, Ontario N5W 5H1

George Brown College
P.O. Box 1015, Station B
Toronto, Ontario M5T 2T9

Georgian College
825 Memorial Ave.
P.O. Box 2316
Orillia, Ontario L3V 6S2

John Abbott College
Box 2000, Ste. Anne
De Bellevue, Quebec H9X
3L9

Niagara College
300 Woodlawn Rd.
P.O. Box 1005
Welland, Ontario L3B 5S2

St. Clair College
2000 Talbot Road W.
Windsor, Ontario N9A 6S4

University of Alberta
Rm. 3032 Dent./Pharmacy
Bldg.
Edmonton, Alberta T6G 2N8

University of Manitoba
780 Bannatyne Ave.,
Rm. D-35
Winnipeg, Manitoba R3E
0W2

Vancouver Community College
250 W. Pender
Vancouver, British Columbia
V6B 1S9

Wascana Institute, Siast
4635 Wascana Pkwy.,
Box 556
Regina, Saskatchewan
S4P 3A3

MASTER'S LEVEL DENTAL HYGIENE PROGRAMS

Medical College of Georgia
School of Graduate Studies
CB-1801
Augusta, GA 30912
Degree Awarded: M.S./
M.H.E. Dental Hygiene

Old Dominion University
Hirschfeld School of Dental
Hygiene
College of Health Sciences
Hampton & 46th
Norfolk, VA 23529-0499
Degree Awarded: M.S. Dental
Hygiene

Texas A&M University System
Baylor College of Dentistry
Caruth School of Dental
Hygiene
P.O. Box 660677
Dallas, TX 75266-0677
Degree Awarded: M.S. Dental
Hygiene (tracks in
education and
administration)

University of Maryland
Department of Dental
Hygiene
666 W. Baltimore St.,
Rm. 3-G-3
Baltimore, MD 21201-1586
Degree Awarded: M.S. Dental
Hygiene

University of Medicine &
Dentistry of New Jersey
School of Health Related
Professions
1776 Rariton Rd., Rm. 425
Scotch Plains, NJ 07076
Degree Awarded: M.S. Health
Science with options for
electives in the Allied
Dental Education Core

University of Michigan
Department of Dental
Hygiene
School of Dentistry
1011 N. University
Ann Arbor, MI 48109-1078
Degree Awarded: M.S. Dental
Hygiene

University of Missouri-Kansas
City
School of Dentistry
Division of Dental Hygiene
Education
650 E. 25th
Kansas City, MO 64l08-2795
Degree Awarded: M.S. Dental
Hygiene

University of Nebraska Medical
Center
Department of Dental
Hygiene
College of Dentistry
40th and Holdrege
Lincoln, NE 68583-0740
Degree Awarded: M.S. offered
through College of
Dentistry

University of North Carolina
Dental Hygiene Education
Master of Science Degree
Program
UNC-School of Dentistry
367 Old Dental Bldg.,
CB#7450
Chapel Hill, NC 27599-7450
Degree Awarded: M.S. Dental
Hygiene Education

University of Texas
Health Science Center at San
Antonio
Department of Dental
Hygiene
7703 Floyd Curl Dr.
San Antonio, TX 78284-7904
Degree Awarded: MS Dental
Hygiene

University of Washington
   B-224 Health Sciences Bldg.,
      SB-22
   Seattle, WA 98195
   Degree Awarded: M.S. Oral
      Biology for Dental Health
      Educators

West Virginia University
   Department of Dental
      Hygiene
   Health Sciences North
   P.O. Box 9425
   Morgantown, WV 26506-
      9425
   Degree Awarded: M.S. Dental
      Hygiene

ACCREDITED DENTAL ASSISTANT PROGRAMS

U.S. SCHOOLS

Alabama

Bessemer State Technical
College
Highway 11 S
P.O. Box 308
Bessemer, AL 35021

Council Trenholm State
1225 Air Base Blvd.
Montgomery, AL 36108

James H. Faulkner State
Community College
Highway 31
Southbay Minette, AL 36507-
2619

John Calhoun State Community
College
P.O. Box 2216
Decatur, AL 35609-2216

Wallace State Community
College
P.O. Box 2000
Hanceville, AL 35077-2000

Alaska

University of Alaska
Dental Programs–AHS Bldg.
3211 Providence Dr.
Anchorage, AK 99508-8371

Arizona

Phoenix College
1202 W. Thomas Rd.
Phoenix, AZ 85013

Arkansas

Pulaski Technical College
3000 W. Scenic Dr.
N. Little Rock, AR 72118-
3399

California

Cerritos College
11110 E. Alondra Blvd.
Norwalk, CA 90650

Chaffey Community College
5885 Haven Ave.
Rancho Cucamonga, CA
91737-3002

Citrus College
1000 W. Foothill
Glendora, CA 91740

City College of San Francisco
50 Phelan Ave.
San Francisco, CA 94112

College of Alameda
555 Atlantic Ave.
Alameda, CA 94501

College of Marin
College Ave.
Kentfield, CA 94904

College of the Redwoods
Tompkins Hill Rd.
Eureka, CA 95501

College of San Mateo
1700 W. Hillsdale Blvd.
San Mateo, CA 94402

Contra Costa College
2600 Mission Bell Dr.
San Pablo, CA 94806

Cypress College
9200 Valley View St.
Cypress, CA 90630

Diablo Valley College
321 Golf Club Rd.
Pleasant Hill, CA 94523

East L.A. Occupational Center
2100 Marengo St.
Los Angeles, CA 90033

Foothill College
12345 El Monte Rd.
Los Altos Hills, CA 94022

Hacienda–La Puente Adult Ed.
15540 E. Fairgrove Ave.
La Puente, CA 91744

Modesto Junior College
435 College Ave.
Modesto, CA 95350

Monterey Peninsula College
980 Fremont Ave.
Monterey, CA 93940

Orange Coast College
2701 Fairview Rd.
Costa Mesa, CA 92628-0120

Palomar Community College
1140 W. Mission Rd.
San Marcos, CA 92069

Pasadena City College
1570 E. Colorado Blvd.
Pasadena, CA 91106

Sacramento City College
3835 Freeport Blvd.
Sacramento, CA 95822

San Diego Mesa College
7250 Mesa College Dr.
San Diego, CA 92111-4999

San Jose City College
2100 Moorpark Ave.
San Jose, CA 95128

Santa Rosa Junior College
1501 Mendocino Ave.
Santa Rosa, CA 95401-4395

Colorado

Emily Griffith Oppor School
1250 Welton St.
Denver, CO 80204

Front Range Community
College
Larimer Campus
P.O. Box 270490
Fort Collins, CO 80527

Front Range Community
College
3645 W. 112th Ave.
Westminister, CO 80030

Pikes Peak Community College
5675 S. Academy Blvd.
Colorado Springs, CO 80906-
5498

Pueblo Community College-DA
900 W. Orman Ave.
Pueblo, CO 81004

T.H. Pickens Techical Center
500 Airport Blvd.
Aurora, CO 80011

Connecticut

Albert I. Prince Regional
Vocational–Technical
500 Bookfield St.
Hartford, CT 06106

Briarwood College
2279 Mount Vernon Rd.
Southington, CT 06489

Eli Whitney Regional
Vocational–Technical
School
71 Jones Rd.
Hamden, CT 06514

Tunxis Community–Technical
College
271 Scott Swamp Rd.
Farmington, CT 06032-3187

Windham Regional
Vocational–Technical
School
1210 Birch St.
Willimantic, CT 06226

Florida

Brevard Community College
1519 Clearlake Rd.
Cocoa, FL 32922

Broward Community College
3501 SW. Davie Rd.
Ft. Lauderdale, FL 333141

Charlotte Vocational–Technical
Center
18300 Toledo Blade Blvd.
Port Charlotte, FL 33948-
3399

Daytona Beach Community
    College
1200 International Speedway
Daytona Beach, FL 32114

D.G. Erwin Technical Center
2010 E. Hillsborough Ave.
Tampa, FL 33610

Gulf Coast Community College
5230 W. Highway 98
Panama City, FL 32401-1058

Indian River Community
    College
3209 Virginia Ave.
Ft. Pierce, FL 34981-5599

Lindsey Hopkins Technical
    Educational Center
750 NW. 20th St.
Miami, FL 33127

Lorenzo Walker Institute of
    Technology
3702 Estey Ave.
Naples, FL 33942-4498

Manatee Technical Institute
5603 34th St. W
Bradenton, FL 34210

Orlando Technical Center
301 W. Amelia St.
Orlando, FL 32801

Palm Beach Community College
4200 Congress Ave.
Lake Worth, FL 33461

Pensacola Junior College
5555 W. Highway 98
Pensacola, FL 32507

Pinellas Technical Education
    Center
901 34th St. S
St. Petersburg, FL 33711

Robert Morgan Vocational–
    Technical Institute
18180 SW. 122nd Ave.
Miami, FL 33177

Santa Fe Community College
3000 NW. 83rd St.
Gainesville, FL 32606

Southern College
5600 Lake Underhill Rd.
Orlando, FL 32807

Tallahassee Community
    College–DA
444 Appleyard Dr.
Tallahassee, FL 32304

Traviss Technical Center
3225 Winter Lake Rd.
Lakeland, FL 33803

Georgia

Albany Technical Institute
1021 Lowe Rd.
Albany, GA 31708

Augusta Technical Institute
3116 Deans Bridge Rd.
Augusta, GA 30906

Gwinnett Technical Institute
1250 Atkinson Rd., Box 1505
Lawrenceville, GA 30246-
1505

Lanier Tech./Gainesville College
P.O. Box 58
Oakwood, GA 30566

Medix School
2108 Cobb Pkwy.
Smyrna, GA 30080

Savannah Technical Institute
5717 White Bluff Rd.
Savannah, GA 31499

Idaho

Boise State University
1910 University Dr.
Boise, ID 83725

Illinois

Elgin Community College
1700 Spartan Dr.
Elgin, Il 60123

Illinois Valley Community
College
815 N. Orlando Smith Ave.
Oglesby, IL 61348-9691

John A. Logan College
Rural Route 2
Carterville, IL 62918

Kaskaskia College
27210 College Rd.,
Centralia, IL 62801

Lewis & Clark Community
College
5800 Godfrey Rd.
Godfrey, IL 62035

Morton College
3801 S. Central Ave.
Cicero, Il 60804

Parkland College
2400 W. Bradley
Champaign, Il 61821

Indiana

Indiana Univ.–Medical Center
Dept. of Periodontics and
Allied Dental Programs
School of Dentistry
1121 W. Michigan St.
Indianapolis, IN 46202-5186

Indiana University Northwest
3223 Broadway
Gary, IN 46409

Indiana University–Purdue
University
2101 Coliseum Blvd.
Eastfort Wayne, IN 46805

Indiana University–South Bend
1700 Mishawaka Ave.
South Bend, IN 46634

Ivy Tech State College
3101 S. Creasy Lane
Box 6299
Lafayette, IN 47903-6299

Professonal Careers Inst.
7302 Woodland Dr.
Indianapolis, IN 46278

University of Southern Indiana
8600 University Blvd.
Evansville, IN 47712

Iowa

Des Moines Area Community
College
2006 Ankeny Blvd.
Ankeny, IA 50021

Hawkeye Community College
1501 E. Orange Rd., Box 8015
Waterloo, IA 50704

Iowa Western Community
College
2700 College Rd., Box 4C
Council Bluffs, IA 51502-
3004

Kirkwood Community College
6301 Kirkwood Blvd. SW.,
Box 2068
Cedar Rapids, IA 52406

Marshalltown Community
College
3700 S. Center St.
Marshalltown, IA 50158

Northeast Iowa Community
College
10250 Sundown Rd.
Peosta, IA 52068

Scott Community College
500 Belmont Rd.
Bettendorf, IA 52722-5649

Western Iowa Tech Community
College
P.O. Box 5199
4647 Stone Ave.
Sioux City, IA 51102

Kansas

Flint Hills Technical School
3301 W. 18th Ave.
Emporia, KS 66801

Salina Area Voc.–Tech. School
2562 Scanlan Ave.
Salina, KS 67401

Wichita Area Technical College
324 North Emporia
Wichita, KS 67202

Kentucky

Central Kentucky Technical
College
308 Vo.–Tech. Rd.
Lexington, KY 40511

Kentucky Tech–West Campus
P.O. Box 7804
5200 Blandville Rd.
Paducah, KY 42002-7408

Louisiana

Louisiana State University
1100 Florida Ave.
New Orleans, LA 70119

Maine

University College of Bangor
Lincoln Hall
29 Texas Ave.
Bangor, ME 04401-4324

Maryland

Medix School
1017 York Rd.
Towson, MD 21204

Massachusetts

Charles H. McCann Technical
School
Hodges Crossroad
North Adams, MA 01247

Massasoit Community College
900 Randolph St.
Canton, MA 02021

Middlesex Community College
33 Kearney Square
Lowell, MA 01852

Mount Ida College
777 Dedham St.
Newton Centre, MA 02159

Northern Essex Community
College
45 Franklin St.
Lawrence, MA 01840

Quinsigamond Community
College
670 W. Boylston St.
Worcester, MA 01606

Southeastern Technical Institute
250 Foundry St.
South Easton, MA 02375

Springfield Technical
Community College
One Armory Square
Springfield, MA 01105

Michigan

Baker College of Port Huron
3403 Lapeer Rd.
Port Huron, MI 48060

Delta College
University Ctr., MI 48710

Grand Rapids Community
College
143 Bostwick St. NE
Grand Rapids, MI 49503

Lake Michigan College
2755 E. Napier
Benton Harbor, MI 49022

Lansing Community College
P.O. Box 40010
Lansing, MI 48901-7210

Mott Community College
1401 E. Court St.
Flint, MI 48503

Northwestern Michigan College
1701 E. Front St.
Traverse City, MI 49684

Washtenaw Community College
4800 E. Huron River Dr.
Ann Arbor, MI 48106

Wayne County Community
    College
    8551 Greenfield, Rm. 310
    Detroit, MI 48228

Minnesota

Central Lakes College
    501 W. College Dr.
    Brainerd, MN 56401

Century College
    3300 Century Ave. N
    White Bear Lake, MN 55110

Dakota County Technical
    College
    1300 145th St. E
    Rosemont, MN 55068

Duluth Business University, Inc.
    412 W. Superior St.
    Duluth, MN 55802

Hennepin Technical College
    9000 Brooklyn Blvd.
    Brooklyn Park, MN 55445

Hibbing Community College
    2900 E. Beltline
    Hibbing, MN 55747

Lakeland Medical–Dental
    Academy
    1402 W. Lake St.
    Minneapolis, MN 55408

Minneapolis Community &
    Technical College
    1501 Hennepin Ave.
    Minneapolis, MN 55403

Minnesota School of Business
    6120 Earle Brown Dr.
    Brooklyn Center, MN 55430

Minnesota West Community &
    Technical College
    1011 First St. W.
    Canby, MN 56220

Northwest Technical College-
    Bemidji
    905 Grant Ave. SE
    Bemidji, MN 56601

Northwest Technical College-
    DA
    1900 28th Ave. S
    Moorhead, MN 56560-4899

Rochester Community &
    Technical College
    851 30th Ave., SE.
    Rochester, MN 55904

South Central Technical College
    1920 Lee Blvd.
    North Mankato, MN 56002-
    1920

St. Cloud Technical College
    1540 Northway Dr.
    St. Cloud, MN 56303-1240

Mississippi

Hinds Community College
    1750 Chadwick Dr.
    Jackson, MS 39204

Pearl River Community College
5448 U.S. Highway 49 S
Hattiesburg, MS 39401

Missouri

East Central College
Box 529
Highway 50 & Prairie
Dellunion, MO 63084

Nichols Career Center
609 Union St.
Jefferson City, MO 65101

Ozarks Technical Community
College
1923 E. Kearney
P.O. Box 5958
Springfield, MO 65803

Penn Valley Community College
3201 SW. Trafficway
Kansas City, MO 64111-2764

Montana

Montana State University
2100 16th Ave. S
Great Falls, MT 59405

Salish Kootenai College
Box 117
Pablo, MT 59855

Nebraska

Central Community College
P.O. Box 1024
Hastings, NE 68902-1024

Metropolitan Community
College
P.O. Box 3777
Omaha, NE 68103-0777

Mid-Plains Community College
1101 Halligan Dr.
North Platte, NE 69101

Omaha College of Health
Careers
225 N. 80th St.
Omaha, NE 68114-3617

Southeast Community College
8800 O St.
Lincoln, NE 68520

Nevada

Truckee Meadows Community
College
7000 Dandini Blvd.
Reno, NV 89512-3999

New Hampshire

New Hampshire Technical
Institute
11 Institute Dr.
Concord, NH 03301-7412

New Jersey

Atlantic County Voc./Tech. Sch.
5080 Atlantic Ave.
Mays Landing, NJ 08330

Berdan Institute
265 Route 46
Westtotowa, NJ 07512

Camden County College
P.O. Box 200
Blackwood, NJ 08012

Cape May County Technical
Institute
188 Crest Haven Rd.
Cape May Courthouse, NJ
08210

Cumberland County Technical–
Education Center
601 Bridgeton Ave.
Bridgeton, NJ 08302

Dental Studies Institute
23 Just Rd.
Fairfield, NJ 07004

Mercer County Vocational–
Technical School
1070 Klockner Rd.
Hamilton, NJ 08619

Technical Institute of Camden
County
343 Berlin-Cross Keys Rd.
Sicklerville, NJ 08081-9709

University of Medical–Dental of
New Jersey
1776 Raritan Rd., Rm. 405
Scotch Plains, NJ 07076

New York

Columbia University–Dental/
Oral Surgery
630 W. 168th St., P & S Box
20
New York, NY 10032

Monroe Community College
1000 E. Henrietta Rd.
Rochester, NY 14623-5780

New York University Dental
Center
345 E. 24th St.
New York, NY 10010

SUNY Educational Opportunity
Center
465 Washington St.
Buffalo, NY 14203

North Carolina

Alamance Community College
P.O. Box 8000
Graham, NC 27253-8000

Asheville–Buncombe Technical
340 Victoria Rd.
Asheville, NC 28801

Cape Fear Community College
411 N. Front St.
Wilmington, NC 28401-3993

Central Piedmont Community
College
1201 Elizabeth Ave.–Kings
Dr.
Charlotte, NC 28204

Coastal Carolina Community
College
444 Western Blvd.
Jacksonville, NC 28540

Fayetteville Tech. Community
  College
  2201 Hull Rd.
  P.O. Box 35236
  Fayetteville, NC 28303

Guilford Technical Community
  College
  P.O. Box 309
  Jamestown, NC 27282

Rowan–Cabarrus Community
  College
  P.O. Box 1595
  Salisbury, NC 28144

University of North Carolina
  367 Old Dental Bldg., Cb#
  7450
  Chapel Hill, NC 27599-7450

Wake Technical Community
  College
  9101 Fayetteville Rd.
  Raleigh, NC 27603-5696

Wayne Community College
  Caller Box 8002
  Goldsboro, NC 27530

Western Piedmont Community
  College
  1001 Burkemont Ave.
  Morganton, NC 28655

Wilkes Community College
  P.O. Box 120
  Wilkesboro, NC 28697-0120

North Dakota

North Dakota State College of
  Science
  Wahpeton, ND 58076

Ohio

Choffin Career Center
  O.W. Wood St., Box 550
  Youngstown, OH 44501

Cuyahoga Community College
  2900 Community College
  Ave.
  Cleveland, OH 44115

Jefferson Community College
  4000 Sunset Blvd.
  Steubenville, OH 43952

Oklahoma

Metro Tech. Health Careers
  Center
  1720 Springlake Dr.
  Oklahoma City, OK 73111

Rose State College
  6420 SE. 15th St.
  Midwest City, OK 73110

Oregon

Blue Mountain Community
  College
  2411 NW. Carden
  Pendleton, OR 97801

Concorde Career Institute
  1827 NE. 44th Ave.
  Portland, OR 97213

Lane Community College
    4000 E. 30th
    Eugene, OR 97405

Linn-Benton Community
        College
    6500 SW. Pacific Blvd.
    Albany, OR 97321

Portland Community College
    P.O. Box 19000
    Portland, OR 97280-0990

Chemeketa Community College
    4000 Lancaster Dr. NE
    Salem, OR 97309

Pennsylvania

Community College of
        Philadelphia
    1700 Spring Garden St.
    Philadelphia, PA 19130

Harcum College
    750 Montgomery Ave.
    Bryn Mawr, PA 19010

Harrisburg Area Community
        College
    One Hacc Dr.
    Harrisburg, PA 17110-2999

Luzerne County Community
        College
    1333 S. Prospect St.
    Nanticoke, PA 18634-3899

Manor Junior College–DA
    700 Fox Chase Rd.
    Jenkintown, PA 19046-3399

Median School of Allied Health
    125 7th St.
    Pittsburgh, PA 15222-3400

Westmoreland County
        Community College
    400 Armbrust Rd.
    Youngwood, PA 15697-1895

Puerto Rico

University of Puerto Rico
    1st Fl.–Academic Affairs
        Office
    San Juan, PR 00936-5067

Rhode Island

Community College of Rhode
        Island
    Louisquisset Pike
    Lincoln, RI 02865

South Carolina

Aiken Technical College
    P.O. Drawer 696
    Aiken, SC 29802

Florence–Darlington Technical
        College
    P.O. Box 100548
    Florence, SC 29501-0548

Greenville Technical College
    P.O. Box 5616, Station B
    Greenville, SC 29606-5616

Midlands Technical College
    P.O. Box 2408
    Columbia, SC 29202

Spartanburg Technical College
P.O. Drawer 4386–Highway
I-85
Spartanburg, SC 29305-4386

Tri-County Technical College
P.O. Box 587
Pendleton, SC 29670

Trident Technical College
P.O. Box 118067
Charleston, SC 29423-8067

York Technical College
452 South Anderson Rd.
Rock Hill, SC 29730

South Dakota

Lake Area Technical Institute
230 11th St. NE
Watertown, SD 57201

Tennessee

Chattanooga State Technical
Community College
4501 Amnicola Highway
Chattanooga, TN 37406-1097

Concorde Career Institute
5100 Poplar Ave., Suite 132
Memphis, TN 38137

East Tennessee State University
1000 W. E St.
Elizabethton, TN 37643

Tennessee Technology Center
1100 Liberty St.
Knoxville, TN 37919

Tennessee Technology Center of
Memphis
550 Alabama Ave.
Memphis, TN 38105-3604

Volunteer State Community
College
Nashville Pike
Gallatin, TN 37066

Texas

Del Mar College
Baldwin & Ayers Sts.
Corpus Christi, TX 78404

El Paso Community College
P.O. Box 20500
El Paso, TX 79998

Grayson County College
6101 Grayson Dr.
Denison, TX 75020-8299

Houston Community College
1900 Galen
Houston, TX 77030

San Antonio College
1300 San Pedro Ave.
San Antonio, TX 78212-4299

School of Health Care–Air Force
917 Missile Rd.
Sheppard AFB, TX 76311-
2246

Texas State Technical College
3801 Campus Dr.
Waco, TX 76705

Utah

American Institute of Medical–
Dental Techology
1675 N. Freedom Blvd., Bldg.
5a
Provo, UT 84604

American Institute–Med./Dent.
Techology
1067 E. Tabernacle St.
St. George, UT 84770-3046

Davis Applied Technology
Center
550 E. 300 S
Kaysville, UT 84037

Provo College
1450 W. 820 N.
Provo, UT 84601

Vermont

Essex Technical Center
3 Educational Dr.
Essex Junction, VT 05452

Virginia

Computer Dynamics Institute
400 South Witchduck Rd.,
#106
Virginia Beach, VA 23462

J. Sargeant Reynolds
Community College
P.O. Box 85622
Richmond, VA 23285-5622

Old Dominion University
G. W. Hirschfeld School
Norfolk, VA 23529-0499

Tidewater Tech.
1760 E. Little Creek Rd.
Norfolk, VA 23518

Tidewater Technical Peninsula
616 Denbigh Blvd.
Newport News, VA 23602-
4416

Wytheville Community College
1000 E. Main St.
Wytheville, VA 24382

Washington

Bates Technical College
1101 S. Yakima Ave.
Tacoma, WA 98405

Bellingham Technical College
3028 Lindbergh Ave.
Bellingham, WA 98225

Clover Park Technical College
4500 Steilacoom Blvd., SW.
Tacoma, WA 98498-4098

Highline Community College
P.O. Box 98000
Des Moines, WA 98198-9800

Lake Washington Technical
College
11605 132nd Ave. NE
Kirkland, WA 98034

Renton Technical College
3000 NE. 4th St.
Renton, WA 98056

South Puget Sound Community
College
2011 Mottman Rd. SW
Olympia, WA 98512-6292

Spokane Community College
North 1810 Greene St., MS
2090
Spokane, WA 99207

Wisconsin

Blackhawk Technical College
6004 Prairie Rd.
Janesville, WI 53547

Fox Valley Technical College
1825 Bluemound Dr.
Appleton, WI 54913

Gateway Technical College
3520 30th Ave.
Kenosha, WI 53144-1690

Lakeshore Technical College
1290 North Ave.
Cleveland, WI 53015

Madison Area Technical College
3550 Anderson St., Rm. 300f
Madison, WI 53704

Northeast Wisconsin Technical
College
2740 W. Mason St.
P.O. Box 19042
Green Bay, WI 54307-9042

Western Wisconsin Technical
College
400 N. Sixth St., Rm. 408
La Crosse, WI 54601

Wyoming

Sheridan College
3059 Coffeen Ave.
Sheridan, WY 82801

CANADIAN SCHOOLS

Camosun College
3100 Foul Bay Rd.
Victoria, British Columbia
V8P 4X8

College of New Caledonia
3330-22nd Ave.
Prince George, British
Columbia V2N 1P8

College of the North Atlantic
Topsail Road, P.O. Box 1693
St. John's, Newfoundland
A1C 5P7

College of the Rockies
Cranbrook, 2700 College Way
Cranbrook, British Columbia
V1C 5l7

Douglas College
    700 Royal Ave.
    New Westminster, British
        Columbia V3l 5B2

Fraser Valley College
    45600 Airport Rd.,
    Chilliwack, British Columbia
        V2P 6T4

Holland College
    140 Weymouth St.
    Charlottetown, Prince Edward
        Island C1A 4Z1

Keewatin Community College
    P.O. Box 3000
    The Pas, Manitoba R3A 1M7

Malsapina University College
    900 Fifth Ave.
    Nanaimo, British Columbia
        V9R 5S5

Newfoundland Career
    Academy Millbrook Mall
    P.O. Box 71
    Corner Brook, Newfoundland
        A2H 6C3

Northern Alberta Institute of
        Technology
    11762-106th St.
    Edmonton, Alberta T5G 2R1

Nova Scotia Institue of
        Technology
    5686 Leeds St.
    P.O. Box 2210
    Halifax, Nova Scotia B3J 3C4

Okanagan University College
    1000 Klo Rd.
    Kelowna, British Columbia
        V1Y 4X8

Open Learning Agency
    4355 Mathissi Pl.
    Burnaby, British Columbia
        V5G 4S8

Red River Community College
    2055 Notre Dame Ave.
    Winnipeg, Manitoba R3H 0J9

Robertson College
    696 Portage Ave.
    Winnipeg, Manitoba R3G
        0M6

Southern Alberta Institute of
        Technology
    1301-16th Ave.
    Northwest Calgary, Alberta
        T2M 0l4

St. Clair College
    2000 Talbot Rd. W
    Windsor, Ontario N9A 6S4

Vancouver Community College
    250 W. Pender
    Vancouver, British Columbia
        V6B 1S9

Wascana Institute, Siast
    4635 Wascana Pkwy., Box
        556
    Regina, Saskatchewan S4P
        3A3

DENTAL LABORATORY TECHNOLOGY PROGRAMS

Arizona

Pima County Community
    College
2202 W. Anklam Rd.
Tucson, AZ 85709

California

Los Angeles City College
    855 N. Vermont Ave.
    Los Angeles, CA 90029

Pasadena City College
    1570 E. Colorado Blvd.
    Pasadena, CA 91106

Florida

Indian River Community
    College
    3209 Virginia Ave.
    Ft. Pierce, FL 34981-5599

Lindsey Hopkins Tech.–
    Educational Center
    750 NW. 20th St.
    Miami, FL 33127

Mcfatter Voc.–Tech. Center
    6500 Nova Dr.
    Davie, FL 33317

Southern College
    5600 Lake Underhill Rd.
    Orlando, FL 32807

Georgia

Atlanta Technical Institute
    1560 Metropolitan Pkwy. SW
    Atlanta, GA 30310

Gwinnett Technical Institute
    1250 Atkinson Rd., Box 1505
    Lawrenceville, GA 30246-
    1505

Idaho

Idaho State University
  Dental Laboratory Technician,
    Box 8380
  Pocatello, ID 83209-8380

Illinois

Southern Illinois University–
    College of Technical
    Careers
  Code 6615
  Carbondale, IL 62901

Triton College
  2000 N. 5th Ave.
  Nueriver Grove, IL 60171

Indiana

Indiana University–Purdue
    University
  2101 Coliseum Blvd.
  East Fort Wayne, IN 46805

Iowa

Kirkwood Community College
  6301 Kirkwood Blvd. SW,
    Box 2068
  Cedar Rapids, IA 52406

Kentucky

Lexington Community College
  Cooper Dr.–Oswald Bldg.
  Lexington, KY 40506

Louisiana

Louisiana State University
  1100 Florida Ave.
  New Orleans, LA 70119

Massachusetts

Middlesex Community College
  33 Kearney Square
  Lowell, MA 01852

Minnesota

Century College
  3300 Century Ave. N
  White Bear Lake, MN 55110

Nebraska

Central Community College
  P.O. Box 1024
  Hastings, NE 68902-1024

New York

Erie Community College–South
    Campus
  S4041 Southwestern Blvd.
  Orchard Park, NY 14127-
    2199

North Carolina

Durham Technical Community
    College
  1637 Lawson St.
  Durham, NC 27703

Ohio

Columbus State Community
    College
  550 E. Spring St., Box 1609
  Columbus, OH 43215

Oregon

Portland Community College
P.O. Box 19000
Portland, OR 97280-0990

Tennessee

East Tennessee State University
1000 W. E St.
Elizabethton, TN 37643

Texas

School of Health Care–Air Force
917 Missile Rd.
Sheppard AFB, TX 76311-
2246

School of Health Care–Army
917 Missile Rd.
Sheppard AFB, TX 76311-
2246

School of Health Care–Navy
917 Missile Rd.
Sheppard AFB, TX 76311-
2246

University of Texas–Health
Sciences
7703 Floyd Curl Dr.
San Antonio, TX 78284-7914

Virginia

J. Sargeant Reynolds
Community College
P.O. Box 85622
Richmond, VA 23285-5622

Washington

Bates Technical College
1101 S. Yakima Ave.
Tacoma, WA 98405

Wisconsin

Milwaukee Area Technical
College
700 W. State St.
Milwaukee, WI 53233